Butterfly
Thoughts
By
Lorie Troyer

Lorie is a child of God, as any one

of us can be if we choose to.

She loves telling people in an honest way

about a God of love, mercy,

grace and forgiveness.

This is Lorie's second published

book of "thoughts"

she is feeling led to share with you.

Praying you will enjoy

them and God will speak to your heart.

Dedication

Dedicating this book to my

granddaughters, Riley, Adelyn and Hannah.

They all love sugar

much like their Grandma.

And Adelyn LOVES butterflies!

I pray for them every day that

they will grow in Christ to

the sweet person

God wants them to be.

Just like a butterfly.

~ Love, Grandma

INTRODUCTION

This is a book of thoughts to help you think deeper in a simple, honest way. To encourage you to allow God to take you from a cocoon to a beautiful butterfly. To the person God intended you to be.

Table of Contents

More Ocean Thoughts

Chapter 1

More thoughts written by the ocean

in various times of my life.

Always take time to enjoy God's

beautiful creation and praise Him for it!!

Ocean Thought #1

(A Seashell Snob)

Lesson #1: It's OK to be broken.

I am sure you have heard of a "coffee snob" or a "chocolate snob," well I was a "seashell snob." When I walked the beach combing for seashells, I would not pick up just any old seashell; it had to be all black, all white, or grey. Any other color would be tossed to the side. Also, as I pick up those crazy little creatures, I find myself choosing the most beautiful, correct-colored shell with utter excitement, only to find out it is broken or has a flaw of some sort. I would promptly throw it down in disgust that it wasn't perfect. Why did it have to be rough around the edges or have such imperfect marks, or worse yet, be in pieces? Could it have been that it was beaten by the waves, or was it trampled on by some people chatting as they walked the beach, not for one instant thinking about that beautiful little shell under their feet? As I was about to throw a little broken shell down one day, it was as if God said to me, when you were broken, did I throw you aside? I stopped in my tracks and put the shell in my bag, but not before I entertained the thought that perhaps I should put it into a different bag, you know, so it wouldn't ruin the beautiful perfect shells.

How many times have we done this in life? Someone is different. Maybe they dress poorly, or perhaps, they dress too well. They could have had a rough childhood or lived in an area we consider "the bad part of town." They had alcoholic parents, or even worse, they are alcoholics themselves. Perhaps they are homeless, and we, in all our wisdom, assume it is by choice. They might have one too many tattoos or piercings, and so we are ready to write them off before we even hear their story. That day on the beach, as I put the broken shell into my little bag, I understood that God was saying, "It's Ok to be broken. We are all broken in one way or another. I love you as you are, now go and love others as I have loved you."

Thanks be to God for the brokenness in our lives, which has shaped us into the person He would want us to be. To God be the Glory!

~Image by Marv

Ocean Thought #2

(The Dizzy Blonde and the Dead Fish)

Lesson #2: God has a purpose for all of us, and it is different for every season of our life.

Have you ever stood at the edge of the water when the tide comes in? If you just stand there and don't move, it feels as though the earth is moving beneath your feet. Then, if you look down and stare at the water rushing back into the ocean, it can make you dizzy. As I was doing that one day, I noticed all the shells and little fish that were constantly carried onto the beach, only to be hammered back into the ocean. On this day, the waves were huge and beating with great force. As I watched the same items coming in, going out, and coming back in again, it made my head spin. I almost felt sorry for the life they had to endure being at the mercy of the waves. Some shells and even fish would remain on the shore, but on this day, not many would lay still on the shore for long. After getting extremely dizzy from watching this circus of nature, I began to walk the beach. Not far into my walk, I came across a dead fish lying on the shore. I stopped, and at that moment, I realized the lesson for the day. This fish was not meant to lay quietly on the shore with no purpose. It was meant to be in the ocean, and if there were days that it got pummeled by the waves, that was OK because it was the life God intended for it to live.

I am sure it had days of wonder and amazement when it could just swim peacefully in the beauty of the ocean, but then some days were rough when it got swept onto the shore and back out again.

I thought of the times I have been so busy in my life with family, work, and even church that it felt as though I was being tossed about by the waves and really getting nowhere. But then I realized God was saying, this was the purpose I have for you in this season of your life. At one point, I was living with chronic kidney disease for 10 years and waiting for a kidney transplant. That became a completely different season. Before, I wished I could slow down, and suddenly. I was forced to. And after having a successful transplant, it was another completely different season in my life. But as I was walking the beach, God spoke to me in ways I can honestly say I never heard Him speak before. He was telling me that no matter what season we are in, He has a purpose for each one of us. And these last 15-20 years have been learning of His love for me, and now, perhaps my purpose is to share that with you.

Give thanks today for the seasons of your life. Remember, God has a purpose for you, and that purpose can change with every season. Don't be afraid to change with it. To God be the Glory!

~ Images by Lorie

Ocean Thought #3

(But There Is More)

Lesson #3: God sent His Son to wash our sins away. But there is more.

I sat and watched the waves being particularly rough that day, creating white caps as I had never seen before. I got up from my chair and felt led to walk at the edge of where the tide was coming in. Walking along, God was showing me exactly what He wanted me to learn. I stood as the waves came in and watched as the water washed across my sand-covered feet. When it washed over again, and I saw that they were clean. Ok God, I thought, I get it. You sent Your Son to wash me clean of my sins. He said to me, "Yes, that is a big part of it. But there is more."

I looked at my feet, wondering what else there could be to this lesson. I continued to walk, and once again, my feet became covered in sand. Just then, a wave came in and did the same thing, and it washed my feet clean. God said to me, "Do you understand?" I thought, yes, I do. Jesus cleanses us of our sins, and we sin repeatedly; our lives get messed up and dirty, and He will always be there to forgive us and cleanse our sins. But God said, "You are almost there. But there is more." As I watched this process one more time, I realized, I was standing still before God, waiting for Him to speak to me. He said, "That is it. I am always here to make you clean of all your sin, but you must do your part as well. You must come before me and repent, spend time with me, and listen for my voice."

Give thanks to God today for sending His Son, Jesus, to cleanse us from our sins. Pray you will be faithful in doing your part. To God be the Glory!

~Image by Marv

Ocean Thought #4

(Footprints in the Sand)

Lesson #4: We may feel like we are heading in all different directions, but the most important path must lead to God.

I was a photographer by profession. I worked in a photography studio for 18 years, then owned that same studio with my husband for 8 years. So, one of my favorite things to do on the beach was to photograph things that speak to me. As I was walking one day, I came across a whole bunch of footprints in the sand. I photographed it simply because I felt led to. Later as I was looking at that picture, I found it interesting how the footprints weren't going in a straight path as you might think. They were all over the place. Some were heading right, some left and some forward. Seeing this image helped me comprehend all the times I have felt as though I was walking in circles, never quite knowing which way I should go. God completed the picture for me by helping me think about what a mess my life is when I go in too many different directions. I need to follow that one straight, narrow path

He wants me to be on. And He is faithful to lead me if I will allow Him to. Another lesson… unexpectedly learned.

Thanking God today for His direction that keeps us from walking in circles. And for His creative ways to speak to me. To God be the Glory!

~Image by Lorie

Ocean Thought #5

(The Sand Dollar)

Lesson #5: Faith and Finances

I have this secret desire to collect perfect sand dollars. The problem is I have never found one. My husband has found three, and I gave them away to people who I felt would really enjoy them, bringing my collection back to a big fat zero. However, as I was about to walk the beach today, I thought, this is the day. I know I am going to find a perfect sand dollar today.

So, optimistically I started out on the beach with my husband. I even shared my incredible optimism with him. Unfortunately, about an hour later, we returned with only 2 partial pieces of a sand dollar. As my husband so eloquently put it, we found about 50 cents worth. I didn't really understand why I had picked up these pieces. It wasn't what I was looking for by any means. I had no idea why until I sat down to write this evening. God made it clear to me that this was a lesson in finances that I needed to share. I must admit there have been plenty of times when

I thought I would have a certain amount of money and only ended up with about half of what I thought I was going to have. I remember the first time this happened. I tried and tried to figure out how to make it stretch to the amount I really needed, but with no luck. I spent many days trying to figure this out myself, not understanding why all of a sudden, I was in this situation. God brought the reasons to a new light when I had no choice but to put it all in His hands. I will always remember what happened when I did just that. God is an amazing God and is greatly to be praised. That is what I found out. Somehow, the money was there. Was I getting rich? No. Did I suddenly have enough? Absolutely. God tends to remind me quite often that I can't take it with me and that His grace is sufficient for me. All I really need is enough to pay for my commitments, eat, and have a roof over my head. But of course, He already knows that. So, why am I worrying about it? If He knows that, and loves me as I know He does, then my only reason for concern is if I can't have enough money to get what I want, not what I need. However, the funny thing is, when I give it over to God, He always gives us far more than we need. This was a tough lesson to learn, but it is the best Faith building lesson I have ever gone through. And I am so thankful that God has carried me through it.

Be thankful today for the extravagant way God takes care of us and pray for Him to show you how to grow in your faith through your finances. To God be the Glory!

~Image by Lorie

Ocean Thought #6

(The Sea Gull)

Lesson #6: Learning the beauty of not being self-sufficient.

I grew up in a Christian family. I had wonderful parents, but the one thing I have always struggled with was feeling that I shouldn't ask for help...especially financially. I am part of a wonderful, generous community that is always there to help when needed. And until recently, I was one of those on the giving side. But God has brought me through many faith-building events where I had to be on the receiving end. Health issues that led to astronomical medical bills made me recognize the importance of trusting God rather than trusting in what I could store up "in case." I am not saying it is wrong to save your money; of course not. But I am saying that God has, for some reason, brought us through a season where we had to swallow our pride and be willing to allow Him to work through those around us. So, when I was watching this beautiful bird on the beach today, it made me remember how much I can learn from the birds. This sea gull sat patiently on the beach, waiting for the tide to come in so he could eat his lunch. He never doubted that God would provide him with the food he so very much wanted. He wasn't keeping fish back in case it wouldn't be provided someday. He had total and complete faith that God would provide this for him daily. He never wavered, nor did he sit there screaming out that he did not have fish right when he wanted it. He patiently, faithfully, waited for God to send those fish when the tide came in. We can learn so very much from the magnificent birds God has created. Patience, strong faith, and total reliance on God are important lessons worth learning.

Thanking God today for providing what we need, whether it be through our own means or through those God sends to help us. To God be the Glory!

~Image by Lorie

Ocean Thought #7

(The Storm and the Sea)

Lesson # 7: We can always find beauty in the middle of our storms.

One of the most beautiful things to behold is a storm brewing over the ocean. All of nature is in harmony, and suddenly, the clouds, the waves, the wind, and even sometimes the sun are all fighting to get the most attention. But when the rain makes its grand entrance, it wins. The beauty of seeing those little raindrops fiercely hit that magnificent body of water with no fear is a remarkable sight.

As I stood inside and watched this magnificent symphony, I had to think about the times I have had a storm brewing up in my life and how God was able to show me the beauty that could come of it. I have had a tremendous number of things happen in my life that have hit me with such force, just like those raindrops on the ocean. But, like the day I stood and watched the sea storm… when I took a step back and watched God orchestrate my little "symphony," it was a beauty to behold. I have wondered so many times why this incredible director of the universe would care about me and my insignificant life. Then God, once again, reminds me how He sent His son for me. And if I were the only person on the earth, He would have done the same thing for me alone. Sometimes it is so easy to go along and forget that during this beautiful mess, we call our lives. When events happen out of our control, and God lifts His wand and turns our problems into an elaborate worship song, I live in amazement. As I look back on the events in my life, I cannot help but lift my voice, my hands, and my heart to God in praise. He has given me so much beauty in the middle of my storms.

Today lift your heart in praise and thanksgiving to God for all He has done in your life. The beauty He has given you and even the problems He has helped you through. God is great and greatly to be praised. To God be the Glory!

~Image by Lorie

Ocean Thought #8

(The Christian Fish in the Sand)

Lesson # 8: Let's be aware not to miss the visuals God puts in front of us that can give us life. Also, we need to be aware of the opportunities God gives us to bring life to someone else.

I was getting ready to leave the beach one day when I saw it. This amazing little creation God made just for me. It was a display of vining flowers that created an almost perfect Christian "fish" symbol. I stood and looked at it a bit to make sure I wasn't imagining it. I photographed it, and when I looked at the image, it was clear this was the formation the vines were creating. I thought to myself how many unusual ways God reminds us of His love. This, to me, was a very creative way! I had walked past this area probably three times before that day and never noticed it. But this time, my eyes were drawn right to it. As I looked at it, I wondered how many people also walked right past it and never noticed it. Or were there others like me whom God felt needed to see a ray of hope in their life and be reminded of His love? God puts many visual things in my path every day. Unfortunately, I know I miss many of them. I also know He gives me opportunities every day to give life to someone else, just as that "fish in the sand" did for me. How many of these have I missed as well? Many, I am sure. I feel I'm always in a hurry…too busy with "important" stuff (to me). But today is a new day and God is calling me to be more aware of those chances He puts in front of me, to be that symbol of a "Christian fish" in the sand and give life to others.

Praise to God for the visuals He gives us that bring a burst of life to us every day. Praying I will also be more aware of how I can bring life to others. To God be the Glory!

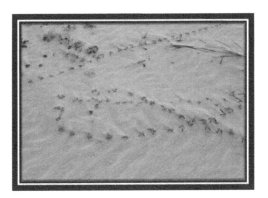

~Image by Lorie

Growing With God

Chapter 2

As a Mom & Grandma,

I have to learn to put

my entire family in

God's care. Praying every day

for them to come

to know God.

Calm Me Down

Do you ever overreact when you hear something is going to happen that you do not want? I am very guilty of this. I had something like that happen this morning. I was so upset. I called Marv. I called my sister. I called a dear friend. Then I prayed. While all the people I reached out to, listened, and tried to help me, I should have prayed first! God helped me calm down. He helped me put it in perspective. He encouraged me to wait and see what happens. To be thankful for what I have and try to find other options to make things work out peacefully. Finally, my heart stopped racing, and my complaining turned to gratitude for all God has done for us. I don't know why reacting negatively to things we don't like is a normal response, but I certainly have that human trait. Once I stopped, prayed, and stepped back, I could see other ways to make it work out fine. It just was not our first plan. Also, God reminded me in His gentle way…Blessed are the peacemakers. I want to be a peacemaker. So… I will pick up my jaw, carry on, and make things work out with God's help. I am so grateful I could turn to God to calm me down. To God be the Glory!

My Dear Lord,

Thank you for always being there to hear my ranting about my big and little worries in a day. And thank you for knowing how to calm my heart. You are the best listener I could ever have. You not only listen, but you have solutions.

In Your Name,

Amen

Having a friend to talk to is great, but talking to God first is the best option!

A Headband and a Tutu

Do you ever wonder why God puts us through challenging times? Why me? Why this? Why now? I have asked those questions many times in my life. But I have learned that God has so much to teach me. And when things are "perfect," it is easy to think I can do it alone. I can take credit for the things when they go well. Am I rich in money? Nope. Not my definition of success. Am I rich in God's blessings? Absolutely. That is the only "success" I need. The kind that requires me to put all my faith in God working things out in my life. And the good news is... He has not failed me yet. And I know He never will. He is faithful. Always. Period. But I have learned it is always in His perfect timing. That is where I learn patience. (And I am still working on this!)

I am so grateful God sees me as a person worth working on, and for the difficult times and all the miracles He has shown me through them. I have learned it is possible to have nothing yet have everything. To God be the Glory!

Dear Lord,

Thank you for giving me all I need in this life. I am so grateful for your amazing grace, love, and the gift of your beautiful son. That is truly enough for me.

In Your Sweet name,

Amen

Sometimes all we need to be happy is a headband and a tutu… and of course, Jesus.

Touch My Boxes, God

Do you ever feel like you are stuck in a box? And if you stay there long enough, it can become a coffin! I know I have times like that! I once heard a pastor telling a story of when Jesus touched the coffin (or box) of a boy who died, and he came back to life. I want God to touch the boxes in my life that are holding me back. Those that are making me lifeless. I heard the pastor say, Jesus did not touch the boy, He touched the box that did not allow him to move. I long for God to touch my stifling boxes and bring me back to life.

There is my "busy box," which happens a lot. I get stuck in there doing things over and over like a robot, just thinking tomorrow will be different. Touch my "busy box," Lord. There is my "pity box." You know, the one where I wonder why I don't have all the amazing things someone else has. Or why did I have to have a kidney transplant? Why me? God, touch that debilitating box for me... please. What about the "tired box"? I have found out I don't do well anymore when I'm tired. I used to push through anything. But I cannot do that anymore. Please, Lord, touch my "tired box." Give me energy or at least the understanding of where I am in life! Then there is the "I'm not good enough box." That is a hard box to live in. I can easily talk myself out of anything by saying I am not good enough to deserve that. Please.... please God, touch this life-sucking box for me.

I could go on and on about all the boxes I have found myself in over the years. But I can also go on about the times God has touched many of those boxes and brought me out of them! I am thankful that God thinks I'm worth Him touching my life debilitating boxes to set me free when needed... so I can enjoy all the glorious, amazing things life has to offer! To God be the Glory!

~Image by Lorie

The Tongue

I heard an interesting sermon once on this most important part of our body. It is not big. It is not the prettiest. We do not have to try to eat more protein to make it stronger. We really do not even have to think about it much. But it sure is powerful…our tongue. What other part of our being can we use so effortlessly and do so much damage or so much good? With a slip of the tongue, we can make someone's day turn sour. Or, with a thoughtful word of encouragement, we can lift someone up when needed. But what really hit me today was no matter how hard we try; we will never be able to control it... without God. This idea of my inability to control my tongue just blows me away. But how often have I tried to control a situation with my unleashed tongue? And it usually turns out badly. Without God, our brains and our emotions control our tongues. But if we have asked God into our hearts, it allows Him to help control what we say and when we say it through our hearts. It is quite a magnificent concept. And one worth thinking through. There are so many relationships ruined every day because of someone's words. I am, of course, guilty of messing up also. I think if we are honest, we have all been guilty of that at some point in our lives. God and my husband have been working on me for years to think about how I say something before I say it. Not an easy concept for me. But one I certainly need to work on. As for our right to freedom of speech... that is a right we don't want to lose. But I am encouraging us, as Christians, to use that right wisely. Not to lash out at others because we feel strongly about a cause. But to take a step back and look at the whole picture before we speak, and envision the outcome if we do not say things in a way that God would want us to. Something to consider...If God is not controlling our words, in person, on social media, and everywhere we go, it will not end well. I can say that from experience. At least it will not be what God would have had us say. Is anyone else feeling the nudge to allow God to control our words? Let's not allow the "cat to get our tongue." I am praying I will be able to give that control to God. I would venture to say the world would be a better place if we all did. To God be the Glory!

Dear Lord,

Please control my tongue for me. I know I cannot do this on my own. Thank you for forgiving me for the times I spoke too quickly or too harshly. Tame my tongue so it glorifies You, Lord.

In Your Precious Name,

Amen

~Image by Adrienne

Shackles and Chains

What are the chains holding you back? I heard someone once talk about how God broke the shackles off Paul when he was imprisoned. He did not take the chain and pull it from the floor. He broke the large metal shackle!! What an incredible God we have! This made me think of all the things in my life that hold me back from being the person I should be. And the reality that God can truly break those chains in my life if I only let Him. I often wonder what these "shackles and chains" could be. It is a fact that we all have something that overpowers our time with God. It could be spending time with people that are influencing us to do things that are "dark", rather than us shining our light of Jesus on them to change their lives. It could be something we choose to do in our own life that is stopping us from doing what God would have us do. It could be any number of things. But God knows all of it. He knows our hearts and our minds. He knows our shackles and our chains. And yet, He lets us choose. He lets us have free will to decide how to live our lives. Of course, He wants us to choose Him over everything else, but can you imagine if we had a God who expected us to be perfect when we accepted Him as our Savior? Or if He expected that we would immediately do no wrong when we said yes to His amazing love? Wow. None of us would be saved, at least not for long. But God, in his amazing ways, walks with us on our journey. He allows us a journey, not one time and you are in…and then you're out because you couldn't live up to His expectations. He patiently waits as we walk through this life and slowly become more like Him. At least, that is how He has worked in my life. And for that, I am forever grateful. Here is to breaking one chain at a time with God by my side. And to not stressing out over everything! To God be the Glory!

Dear Lord,

Thank you for giving me a second, third and more chances in my life than I ever deserve. Help me to remember that without You, I am nothing. My life would be dark and short. I am so grateful you have given me the choice to spend eternity with You.

In Your Holy Name,

Amen

Shackles represent what we don't want to do…

Chains are what keep us stressed!

LETS BREAK ALL OF THEM!!

Servant Thoughts

God calls us to serve others. To reach out to those in need. I am not trying to sound bitter, but I must admit I have been "burned" a few times when doing that for someone. Times when I have given everything I could to help someone, only to be shunned by them because I did not do enough in their eyes. Or realizing when all was said and done, they were just manipulating me. Not really trying to change their life at all. No matter what was done for them, there was always more that was "needed." And it is easy to become hardened to help anyone again.

So, God was speaking to me in my devotional this morning. He knows I have struggled with some people I have helped. BUT… we are called to help people. Period. I may never see the result for that person. I may never know why I was called to do it. I may not feel the gratefulness from them I am so sure I deserve! And I may be made to feel like I just did not do enough. However, today God reminded me that HIS EYES are the only ones that matter. How he sees my heart while I am trying to help someone is what is important. And if I am doing it with a servant's heart, then it is not only enough, but it is also His will. If I fall short of doing everything that they feel I should have done, that's ok. Because I did what God led me to do. This is especially important for me to remember. Because as a human, if it were up to me, I could easily say I am never helping anyone again. But God... God does not see me through their eyes. He sees me through His eyes. And if I am following his nudge to help someone, that's enough. I will never have to answer why that person did this or that. I never have to feel like I was an enabler to help them get what they wanted and then go back to their old ways. They will have to answer to God for that... not me.

Something that is easy for me to struggle with is people who stand by the side of the road asking for money. My heart breaks for them. I don't know their story. There is a saying, "We are all just one paycheck away from being homeless." So, I typically want to help them because that could be me someday! But I don't always stop because I can justify in my mind ... they may use it for drugs or alcohol. Why should I give them my money to do that? But God... BUT GOD! If I feel a nudge to help one of them... then I need to do it. That is what God has asked of me. Period. I do not need to know if they used that money for food or alcohol. I am simply giving them another chance to be grateful. Another chance for God to work on their heart. I have done what God asked of me. Maybe God will somehow reach them because of what I did. I will never know. And that is ok. God will know. Do I need to stop for everyone by the side of the road? No. Just those that God puts on my heart. So today, I am remembering that God sees me through His eyes only. Not the eyes of the person I am helping. And that makes all the difference in the world to me. Will I help someone again? Yes. If God leads me to do so. Will I get "burned"? Possibly. Will God see my heart through my actions to follow His nudging? Absolutely. Is that enough for me? You bet it is. I am living for an audience of one. Helping someone may seem ridiculous at the time. But if God is nudging me to do it, you can bet it has a purpose. And if I never see what that is, it's ok. I am only answering to what God asked me to do. Period. Nothing more. Nothing less. To God be the glory.

Dear Lord,

Help me to remember how you helped me even when I did not deserve it. And if I get to the point where you are saying…now you are enabling them, please help me to walk away. Because then it is not only OK, but also Your will. Help me to remember You always have a reason to put someone in my path, even if I cannot see the result.

In your Name,

Amen

However, sometimes God lets us feel the appreciation…

What a blessing!

Only Jesus

If you know me at all, you know how much I like to listen to contemporary Christian music. So, sometimes at night I turn this music on to help me go to sleep. Last night I woke up to go to the bathroom. When I got all snuggled back in bed, this song came on and it caught my attention. I have heard it before, but for some reason I couldn't go back to sleep until I heard it all. The name is "Only Jesus" by Casting Crowns. It made me think of all the times my entire life revolved around being "somebody." Making a name for myself in photography or whatever was important to me at the time. As I listened to this song, I very happily realized that the "all about me desires" are no longer me. God has changed my heart to want to put Him first.

I am not going to lie. There are times I do not feel good, and it may seem I have slipped back into "me" mode. However, I can honestly say it's only because I know if I take care of myself and rest, then I'll feel better again. And I am not only ok with that, I believe it is what God would want me to do. But overall, as the song says, I do not care if people remember me, my photographs, or my writings. I just want them to come to know Jesus and remember His name. I am not saying this to sound like I am perfect.

Never. I have a lot to learn. But I am saying it because that is what matters... only Jesus. And this is one area I think God has profoundly changed me. I appreciate it when something I write touches someone. And, of course, I appreciate it when they let me know that. But that is not why I am writing my thoughts. I am writing them because if they bring even one person to Jesus, if one person realizes the importance of that all-mighty name... Jesus. Then it is all good. Then what I wrote gave Him glory. This is what the artist singing "Only Jesus" was trying to say. Someone remembering our names is nice, but if we can bring others to remember Jesus's name, then we have done what God asks of us. To share this wonderful life that He has offered to us. I can only hope I can do God justice in my writings. To God be the Glory!

My Dear Lord,

Thank you for giving me the opportunity to write. Help me to always give You the glory in all I say. In Your Sweet Name,

Amen

Heart Thoughts

I have heard of writer's block. But for the past few days, I think I have been experiencing it. For those of you who know me, a lack of words does not happen often! So, I was sitting here thinking, what is wrong with me? Almost any day of the week, I could write a dozen "thoughts" of various kinds. But these last few days, it was as if my mind was not coordinated with my fingers. As I was sitting out here on our porch today, listening to my wind chimes and the birds, and feeling the breeze on my face, it started returning. Then it hit me.

When I write, I truly just write from my heart. The English may not be perfect, but the message is real. And I was thinking, since the 2020 quarantine is over, how busy I have been again. Truthfully, I simply cannot write when my mind is on a hundred different subjects. My "heart thoughts" just cannot come out. I keep asking myself why I slowed down and stayed home because the government told me to. Is that really when I chose to slow down? And I was the first to go out as soon as they said we can. We were all told you can only have ten people at a gathering. People cancelled family things because of that. Like that 11th person was the one who was going to bring in the virus? And my heart goes out to those not allowed to properly grieve their loved ones deaths. But, of course, protesting is encouraged. This is not, for me, a political statement. It is simply an acknowledgment of what has happened. I had to really think about this! Even when a complete shutdown sounded so absurd to me, I listened because I heard the voices of those in charge say I should. Then I thought, what a concept! I say that I have put God in charge of my life. But have I totally?

How often does God say to me I should do something, and guess what? I think it sounds absurd. And when I try to relay that thought to others for advice, I soon realize I sound a little crazy. So, I don't do it. And yet, when this entire world of humans said, "Stay home," I promptly did it. No matter how absurd it sounded. I do not personally believe we should have done that, but it is interesting how I jumped on the bandwagon because everyone was doing it. If you are a Christian, you are aware of God's upside-down kingdom. I completely get this concept. And if I truly look back on my life and look at the decisions that I made that were safe and "normal," they are not the ones that ever changed my life. But when I truly felt God was leading me to do something "absurd," and I did it,

He never let me down. God is all-knowing and all-seeing, so why would I, as a mere human, think my ideas were better than His? Well, I think it could be because I rely too much on others' advice, rather than His voice leading me. And some of God's ideas are just too out there for loved ones to say... go ahead and do that crazy thing! How could someone choose to leave everything behind to follow him and minister to a third-world country? How could someone choose to give up a promotion with a pay raise just because the company's policies are not morally right? I mean, everyone cheats a little. Everyone lies sometimes. I need the money! Right? So, doesn't that make it ok? I am sure in God's mind; it is not OK. And while the reward may not come in the form of money right now, the reward in Heaven is far better and worth the hard choice. Today I am praying I can learn to make the hard choices God leads me to make. I wonder how different my life would have been if I had done this sooner. All I can know for sure is that every time I made the easier choice, God was still there to walk me through my mistakes. For that, I am thankful. His grace is utterly amazing. And I have no reason to be afraid to do the "absurd'!! If it is God's voice telling me to! To God be the glory!

My Dear Lord,

Please help me to follow Your will in my life. To not shy away from doing what You ask of me just because those around me may not understand it, or because I think it is just too hard. Thank you for Your guidance and love in all my life, even when I don't do what You ask.

In Your Amazing Name,

Amen

DON'T BE AFRAID TO DO THE HARD THING!

~Image by Marv

God's Will

I do not know about you, but sometimes I struggle to understand God's will for my life. I heard a pastor say once that we should pray confidently for everything we want and need. And then pray, God I want what your will is for my life; if any of that I prayed for is not your will, then please do not give it to me.

A light bulb went off in my head! If my heart genuinely wants to live in God's will (and sometimes it's just plain hard to understand what that is), this makes total sense. I trust God; I trust He wants what is best for me. I know that God understands what is best for me far better than I can even begin to know. So, if my heart is in tune with God, I can confidently pray for the desires of my heart. Even things I may view as silly to ask God for. Because if we honestly want to do God's will, and we voice that to Him, he will only give us what He knows is best for us. But when our heart is not lined up with God, and we ask for things that we know aren't good for us, well ...God can either allow them to happen to help us learn and become in tune +with Him, or we will just live in chaos because we will find a way to get what WE want. I don't know if this makes as much sense to you as it did to me, but it was quite an "aha" moment for me when I heard this. It took the pressure off me trying to always understand God's will and helped me realize that God knows and always wants what is best for me. All He asks is that I align my heart with Him. And He will hear all my requests and grant a yes, or no answer based on His will for my life at that very moment. It is such a relief to remember God truly has this thing called life. To God be the glory!

Dear Lord,

Thank you for giving me what is best for me. If I ask for something that will not be good for me, or not help me to learn, I know You will answer with a NO. I am grateful for that, and for Your unchanging love for me.

In Your Name,

Amen

Whatever the answer Lord, help me understand.

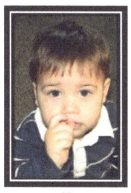

Challenges

Chapter 3

Always be ready.

To walk with

God through

the hard times.

He will open the

doors to bring you

to the mountain top.

~Image by Marv

Blowing Away the Ashes

There is the saying, "Beauty for ashes." I have always loved that saying because it reminds me how God can take something that seems incredibly horrible at the time and turn it into a blessing in our lives. I used to think, how can God take this thing I am going through and make it even OK, let alone a gift? Well, years later, God has shown me how and proven to be faithful in doing just that. I do not know about you, but I have an ash or two in my life that has taken me years to hand over to God. And only when I am willing to give them to Him can He work them out.

There is one thing I have struggled with for many years. I would think it is all OK, I'm forgiven…and then the devil would talk me into believing I was not worthy of being saved…simply because of this one thing. God quietly tells me otherwise, but I must choose to listen to Him, not Satan. Because God truly is on my side and yours. But once again, it is that free will thing God has given us.

One day I had my grandson, Noah, at my house. I was busy doing something else, and he was trying to talk to me, but I was thinking about what I was doing. Finally, he sat down on the floor and threw his hands up! Then he spoke very loudly, "I am trying to tell you something!" I realized he was not being bad by constantly bugging me. He just needed me to listen, and then he was fine. It was not a big deal once he told me what he wanted, and I could quickly help him. I was simply wrapped up in what I wanted to do instead. I was the problem, not him, because I was not really listening to him!

I wonder how often God just throws up His arms when He is trying to tell us something. He assures us repeatedly that if we ask (from our heart) for forgiveness, He will forgive us. Our sins are not seen again by Him. So why is it so hard to honestly believe that? Why can't I believe He will blow all those ashes so far away that we will never see them again? Maybe it's just part of getting older, but I have found the ability to look back on my pile of ashes and know that they have shrunk to nothing is a true blessing. Jesus took all my ashes and has shown me the beauty of living in His light. I am still human, as we all are. And Satan loves to plant that doubt in my head anytime I will allow him to. The challenge is being aware that it is

Satan telling me that. Not God. And knowing in my heart of hearts that I am fully forgiven. My ashes were blown away by Jesus. And God wants us to live in the beauty of knowing Him.

"Beauty for Ashes." Best saying ever because God has shown me that repeatedly. We are so blessed to have a God who forgives! We can rest easy when we genuinely ask for forgiveness, and can believe we are forgiven! And then we can learn to see the beauty that came from our ashes. To God be the Glory!

~Image by Lorie

Circumstances

Have you ever been tested by your circumstances? I am sure almost everyone has. Yesterday started out that way for us. And I want to preface this with, I am not complaining. We feel very blessed to be in Florida, this has been a fantastic trip so far. But sometimes we are tested with just plain frustrating circumstances to see how we react. I am not sure I passed the test, but things got better as the day went on.

We ventured to Key West and made a reservation at Key Largo. However, our reservations got mixed up, and we spent half the day straightening things out. This time the tables were a little turned. Calm and collected Marv was highly frustrated...but excitable, easily frustrated Lorie was able to make calls to finally figure things out. However, I did reach a breaking point once or twice trying to remove an incorrect charge from our account and get the hotel we wanted finally booked. I know this could sound very trivial compared to so many problems today, but sometimes, these little circumstances can get the best of us. Something goes wrong, not because of our own doing, yet we are paying the price for it. But at the time, I remember feeling it would be

OK. I could focus on how lucky we were to be there, and even if it was not going the way we wanted, we were still very blessed. As soon as I was willing to give in to the fact that angry, frustrating actions would do nothing to help the situation, things started changing for the better. I am only telling you this to say that even when we are in a good place in our lives, we must choose not to let things steal our joy. It seems understandable why we may get frustrated during tough times, but we need to remember to give even the most minor things to God. As the day went on, the weather was beautiful. We went kayaking. We relaxed on the dock and saw an amazing sunset. So, what started out to be a crazy day turned into a beautiful one. And none of my joy was stolen. This is a lesson I need to remember. To God be the Glory!

Dear Lord,

Help me to remember to give even the smallest things to You. Please remind me when my attitude turns to frustration and starts to steal my joy that I can give everything to You, even the little aggravations. Thank you for loving me that much!

In Your Most Precious Name,

Amen

Kayaking on the bay at Key Largo

Sunset at Key Largo   ~Image by Marv

Confidence

I used to think that being confident made me seem obnoxious. That was one reason I would often struggle with acting confidently. Then one day, I heard someone speak about this subject, which put everything into perspective. For years I would go back and forth from feeling confident to feeling like everything I do is wrong. And when I would see someone who was highly confident in themselves, it would almost turn me off. It bothered me for years. I did not want to be so sure of myself that I annoyed others. But I wanted to have enough confidence to accomplish things I wanted to do, and that God was leading me to do. So, when I was listening to this speaker, the light bulb came on.

I was struggling because I was trying to have confidence in myself. And just like anyone else, I am just human. There is only so much a human can do correctly. And I could blame my lack of confidence on various other people or mistakes I have made, but that is not right either. I finally realized my confidence could not come from me or other people. It can only come from my choice to put my trust in God. And giving Him the Glory for the successes

He helps me achieve. Being confident is a good thing. But only if it comes from asking God daily to provide me with the strength and confidence to do what He leads me to do. Philippians 4:13 says. "I can do anything through Christ who strengthens me." I have found this to be so true. Only through God's grace can I have the confidence to do anything. I am so thankful for this gift He has made available to any of us. To God be the Glory!

Dear Lord,

Please give me the confidence to do what You want me to accomplish today. Please put in my heart Your desires and give me the strength to carry them through. And to you be the Glory every minute, hour, and day for the accomplishments you give me the confidence to do.

In Your Holy Name,

Amen

Have confidence to try new things!!

~Images by Lorie

The Birds and the Bugs

I have found mowing to be a peaceful "therapy" session. I take my cell phone but do not use it unless it's an emergency. The only noise is the sound of the tractor which is mesmerizing to me. So, it is just me, God, the birds, and the bugs! It is incredible how any time I spend with God can rejuvenate me.

As I was mowing, I had many birds flying right in front of my tractor. They did not fear the loud noise of the tractor. They did not even seem to be concerned about this big machine coming at them! They were on a mission. I wondered how determined they were to get those bugs I was stirring up in the yard. Of course, I had to pull my phone out to try to take a picture of these silly little birds to share with others. That qualifies as an emergency?!

But unfortunately, they were only there if I was moving. When I tried photographing them while driving, it was quite comical and not too smart. I had to imagine if someone was watching me, they would have gotten a good laugh! And as a wise person once said, "If you have a terribly embarrassing moment and it causes someone to smile or laugh, it is OK. At least it was not a wasted moment." I always liked that thought. However, I still did not get that perfect picture!

So, after my photo fiasco, I was moving along thinking about those birds. How hard they worked. They were persistent in doing what they knew they were made to do. And how fearless! As I kept mowing, I felt like God was saying, you need to be that persistent, Lorie. You need to work that hard to do what I have created you to do. And you need to follow Me (God) with fearless abandon! I know for me; I can get distracted quite easily. And I find each day, I must remind myself that the most important thing I will do all day is to show God's love to someone. And to open my ears and heart to His voice to lead me in that direction.

I also know that I can sometimes be afraid to say what God is leading me to say. Will someone think I am trying to be preachy? Will they think I'm acting like I know it all? Will it sound like I am trying to tell them what to do or how to be? Of course, that is never my intention and I pray no one ever feels that way from my writings. However, I realized if God is leading me and giving me the words, He will take those words, do with them what is needed, and reach those who need to hear them. Following God's lead is the most satisfying thing I could ever do. Not because it is me, but because ...it's Him!! To God be the Glory!

~Image by Lorie

Follow God with reckless abandon!!

Doers

What is a doer? I never really thought about it. It is a strange word. But it is someone who does something. Pretty simple, right?

As simple as it sounds, that is how hard it can be to become doers for God. We can read God's word. We can hear God's word. But if we only apply it to being "good people" for our own lives and do not "do" the things God leads us to do, then we fall short…short of God's natural plan for our lives. I don't think God believes or expects us to do it perfectly. He is smarter than that! But He wants to see our best human effort put forth. Sometimes (and if I am being honest…it would be more than that), I struggle to be a doer for God instead of being a doer of what I want to do. I am not saying God expects us to not do things we enjoy. Of course He wants that for us. He created us, so He is fully aware of what we like to do for enjoyment. But He also put us on this earth with a specific plan for each one of us. And only God will know that plan unless we open the eyes of our hearts to see where He will lead us.

There may be someone out there saying, "What in the world is she talking about?" The eyes of our heart? To me, this means when we open our eyes to read or our ears to hear God's word, it helps us allow the Holy Spirit to open our hearts so we can feel how God wants to lead us. If we are willing to do this, He will guide us in the direction He has planned for our life. And that life will be so very fulfilling. But we all must take that first step! To God be the Glory!!!

Take that first step!!!

~ Image by Lorie

"You Say"

I was listening to Lauren Daigle this morning. Her song "You Say" was playing. It struck me how I had spent many years thinking I was not as good as other people. Comparing myself to someone and wondering why my life was not as easy as theirs. Why wasn't I as beautiful as someone else? I have wasted too much time thinking I was weak or not good enough. Or I wasn't rich like other people I know. But as I listened to the words of that song, it reminded me of what I have come to understand. God made me just like He wants me to be. He says I am strong even if I don't feel like it. He says I am good enough. He says I am beautiful just as I am. He says I am rich in ways that cannot be measured with money. And mostly, He thinks I am worthy of His love and forgiveness. Wow! That is true for all of us if we just turn to Him. Without Him, I am nothing. With God, I am unbelievably rich. I hope someone reading this who does not understand that will come to believe it today. You are created exactly as God wants you to be. And do not ever doubt that! To God be the Glory.

Dear Gracious Lord,

Thank You for viewing me as strong, beautiful, rich, and worthy of Your love and forgiveness. That makes this crazy life worth living every day to the fullest. I am so grateful You have proven this to be true. I pray today that many people will have their hearts touched by You so they can also understand this amazing truth... they are worthy. Today I am praying for my family to know they are worthy!

In Your Most Precious Name,

Amen

Recognizing God's Power

Chapter 4

Giving up our control

and power to God

is true freedom.

~Image by Marv

Victory Thoughts

I don't know about you, but I easily become negative when I'm in a challenging situation. It is not long before my thoughts can be...why me? Or what am I supposed to do now? Recently I have been helping with a group of young kids (3–12-year-olds) at our church called Soul Singers. We just enjoy worshipping God. We sing, we laugh, we dance a little. We create relationships. But we also do devotions and prayer requests. It is impressive how many raise their hands to ask for prayer. There are some health requests. There are requests for family. There are also requests for school things. One little girl asked God to shorten the school year!! I explained to her that might not happen, but we could pray that she would have such a fun time it would feel shorter! When a prayer is answered, I highlight it in our prayer book. It is amazing how children will get so excited about the victory of prayers being answered! There is a reason Jesus said, "Let the children come to me." There is so much to learn from them before they get tainted with everything happening around them. I see pure expectation in their eyes when they ask God for help. They do not approach it with an attitude of you probably can't do this, Lord, but this is what I'm asking for. They have unwavering faith that God will answer their prayers. They are, however, just learning God will answer every prayer in His own way, just like the shortening school example. Even though He could have absolutely shorten the school year if it were best for her, that could also bring something along with it that we may not want at all…such as COVID did. But this little girl is learning that God will help us in the best way for us! Maybe by changing HER attitude even if He isn't physically shortening the year. Prayer is a unique gift God has allowed us to have. One I know I often take for granted. God is a "fixer." He is not only willing to walk us through our problems, but he does it with a solution that has our best interests in mind. First, however, we must have faith in His abilities to do just that. Something to think about when praying. Lord, please help us to not fret over things but rather pray like a child who expects victory with every prayer! To God be the Glory!

Struggling

I am struggling with what to do when I'm struggling with what to do. That sounds dumb based on all the ways I have previously written about how to handle different situations. Giving worries to God, listening for His voice, etc. But I am human. I have been avoiding writing for several reasons. I have been busy. That is the first bad excuse. I have not been in the "frame of mind" because of the emotional events I have dealt with lately. I do not think that is a bad excuse... it is reality. God made us with emotions. And sometimes, people do things that hurt us and can turn our worlds upside down. I do not always handle it correctly and I take responsibility for that.

But I was wondering this morning if those who have hurt me are taking the responsibility that is theirs? I turned Joyce Meyer on TV to listen for a while. She just happened to be talking about "Loving those who are hard to love!" She covered several points backed up by scripture. Once again, God knew exactly what I needed to hear at that moment. I only need to answer for what I do. If others do not take responsibility for the way they hurt me, then that's on them. And she did not just cover God's call for us to love those who love us, but she also talked about loving those that hurt us.

I understand this. But if I am being honest, there are some people who are very hard for me to love. I am not proud of myself when I say that, but I realized when I was listening to her that I may not be easy to love either! What? Really? She even went as far as to say that we need to pray for those who have hurt us. And be kind to them. I mean, I have grown up in church all my life. I know this, but when she reminded me of the importance of it, I had to really think about it. She also made it very clear that it doesn't mean we should be a doormat, either. If someone genuinely hurts you, sometimes it requires confronting it, so we don't let it fester and come out wrong. (Which is what I am notorious for) The key is doing it in an effective way. Since I have been on my anti-rejection medicines, I struggle a lot with keeping my emotions in check.

This is not an excuse but a huge reality for me. And I am sorry for the times I have let those emotions show in a way I shouldn't have. But these last few weeks have been a good reminder about this very thing. Stressful situations. Relational issues. Unnecessary things I bring on myself can create those stressful situations. Giving this ALL to God is so important and I am so glad I was reminded of that today. I feel like God has my back and has such a kind way of putting my world back into a good place again. It is like music to my ears! For that, I am thankful. To God be the glory!

~Image by Lorie

Being Stronger

"What doesn't kill you makes you stronger." This is a popular quote. People use it to encourage others in various situations. For instance, if someone is training for a marathon or any physically challenging event, or maybe someone is going through a difficult divorce. Or dealing with an abusive spouse. It could be someone is struggling financially to the point where they have no idea where their next meal is coming from. Maybe it's a hurtful family or close friend relationship. So many things in this life can be just plain hard. I must admit if I have not experienced all of the above, then I have walked through those times with someone who has.

I remember seeing encouraging posters with uplifting sayings on them. Self-help books. Cute little signs to put up in our homes that remind us of good things. I have bought some with the idea of giving myself or someone else a boost of hope. And reading them does make me feel better for a moment. But I have come to realize, to just keep telling myself, "I can do this. I can do this," "I know I can get through this horrible situation," just is not enough. I have found the harder I try to become stronger (on my own) through the tough times, the more frustrated I get. I am not saying we can't feel a sense of accomplishment when we finish something we set out to do. But I still need to recognize God's part in it to give Him the glory. A year before I had my transplant, I rode a bike with our youth group from Dalton, Ohio to Pittsburgh, Pennsylvania for a youth convention. We rode fifty miles a day for three days. It was 90 degrees outside, and my kidneys were only functioning at about 25%. It might not have been the wisest decision I ever made. But it was something I wanted to do to help me get past feeling so "sickly" all the time. Looking back, I don't think I realized what a big role God played, so I could accomplish that. I remember thinking when it was done, "I did it!!" I was feeling pretty good about myself.

But I know it was not just me. God knew how much I needed that in my life right then. Looking at the circumstances, it really made no sense for me to do it because of my kidney situation. And I never really asked the doctor. I was afraid he would say no because the potential to become dehydrated in that heat was high. And that was not a good scenario for my kidneys. I never really hesitated to do it. I prayed for it. I rode my bike every day before to prepare for it. But honestly, I was scared something might happen to me. If it had not been for God riding with me, I never would have made it. And I am thankful to God for giving me that memory. Not to remember how "I did it." But to remind me of God's unending love for me. And how He walks (or rides!) with us through everything. He knew how much it meant to me, and He made sure He was with me every mile of the way. Maybe you are facing a tough situation right now. Relational, financial, or physical. And you feel like you will never be able to get through it.

Or perhaps you have a real sense of accomplishment or even pride that you have done something that seemed rather impossible. Either way, I just want to encourage you to either turn to God to help you through or look back on your accomplishment to see what role God played in that situation. And then give Him the honor and glory He deserves. My life feels like a bunch of short movies. Some are tragedies. Some are mysteries. Some are comedies! In each "movie," the plot is the same. I am faced with an impossible or challenging situation. I try to do it on my own. I get frustrated. I finally turn to God. He leads me through with His deep love for me. And in the end, I can always see how God worked in my life. If I look hard enough, I can even see the humor in most of them!

Whatever you are going through right now, just remember to turn to God and then always give Him the glory He deserves! And at the end of our lives, we will have a beautiful, long movie with God's footprint all over it. So yes, "What doesn't kill you makes you stronger." I just want to challenge us to remember it is not always us who makes us stronger. At least, that's not what I have found to be true. God plays a role in all my situations. And turning to Him … that is what makes me stronger. If we think about it, God plays a role in everything that happens on this earth. To God be the glory!

~Image by Marv

Recovered and Renewed

I rested my knee in bed all day one day, except to go sit on our porch (with my leg up) for a bit during sunset. It was so beautiful outside. I needed to do it to help heal my mind! So, today is another day!! My knee is feeling a little better. I will try to do some things but with much caution. So, this led me to think about recovery. There are so many things we must heal from within our lives. If we really sit and think about it, it could be truly overwhelming! For instance, physically, I have had to recover from a full-body infection of my sinuses that made me horribly sick and put me in the ER about once a month. (Plus, this is what ruined my kidneys). I had to recover from sinus surgery, gallbladder surgery, a hysterectomy, and a kidney transplant. And I am possibly looking at a knee replacement. (But I am praying for a miracle first!) Emotionally, I am still trying to "recover" from all the side effects of my anti-rejection and many other medicines. While I know those side effects will never go away, each day, I try to find ways to deal with them, which is a form of recovery.

Wow! When I list them all out, you are probably amazed Marv is still sticking with me! I have an amazing husband who helps me in many ways I cannot even explain. And for that, I am so thankful. But then, thinking of people around me who have had to deal with far worse events than me, my mind becomes overwhelmed. I know those who have lost parents too young, siblings too young, spouses too young, and maybe worst of all, children too young! How do we recover from all these things in our lives? I think on the physical things, when we recover, we are soon able to forget the pain we went through. But the emotional things are a different matter. And the ones that involve matters of the heart are hard to ever recover from totally. Rather than recovered, the word God brings to my mind is renewed. I know there are some emotional events in my life (other than those related to my meds) that I never really recovered from. But I was renewed after God walked through them with me. The difference is that they will always leave huge scars on my heart, but God has shown me a new way of thinking about them. Rather than dwelling on the horrible thing that happened, I am choosing to realize what I have been able to learn from that event and then how I can use that knowledge to help others. I will never be able to forget they happened because of the hurt they caused, but I am able to deal with them because God has helped me grow through it all.

The old saying when something happens to us, "We either get bitter or we get better," is so true. And God has shown me so many times that being bitter only hurts me. It does not mean I won't feel that hurt or sense of loss ever again, but He has shown me I can do so much more with it if I choose to be better. So, I am grateful for the scars I have because they are a reminder to me that it is not only possible to come out better, but it increased my faith that God has never left me. It is still a process every time something happens. But I am getting better at remembering how faithful God has been in the past. And isn't that really part of our growing in Him? When things happen, we either become better because we have relied on God and have found His faithfulness through it all...or we become bitter because we choose to ignore God and His help in our healing. I am not saying this to be judgmental at all. I have been on both sides. But I have found that going through hurtful things WITH God is so much easier than WITHOUT Him! To put those burdens on His shoulders rather than mine is the only way I know of "recovering". Or, better yet, "renewing" my life to have a better understanding of how to deal with those hurts and increase my faith in God. Another favorite song of mine is "Scars" by "I Am They."

It talks about being grateful for not only our scars that have increased our faith but also being thankful for the scars of Jesus. The scars that changed everything for us. I do not believe Jesus wanted to go through that horrible death, but He knew if he did, He would be making it better for all of us. What a sacrifice. This made me think about recovering or renewing in an even different way yet. I wonder if Jesus has forgotten about this difficult thing He had to go through. I don't think so. But is He bitter about it? I am sure He is not. I want to try to take a lesson from Him. If He can go through the horrible death He went through for us, and come out better rather than bitter, I believe He is asking us to do the same. When I go through things in my life that seem unthinkable, I want to remember the day Jesus went through a painful death for me. And how He handled it. I will never be perfect like Him, but I can try to learn from how He went through it. That is one way I can be renewed. Understanding that no matter what we go through, there is a reason I am going through that. Maybe it is so I can be of help to someone else. Maybe it isn't just all about me. I do not think God would have put His son through that horrible death if it was all about Jesus.

He did it so He could be there for others. I like to think that learning from my hurts can help others go through their hurts, also. That renews my soul! Today I am thankful for my scars and what they remind me of. But I am also so very thankful for the scars of Jesus and what they can mean to all of us! New life! To God be the Glory!

~Image by Marv

Bring the Rain

My husband had off work today, and we decided to venture out this morning. We wanted to look for plants to put in our landscaping and in my planters. It was raining, and I don't think we thought that through. After we broke down and bought two umbrellas, we found a few plants we wanted. But as I was standing out amongst those beautiful plants, I found myself saying, this is ridiculous! Why can't it just stop raining so I can look better? There I go again. Not being thankful for this wonderful rain that was watering all those beautiful plants I was looking at. Nobody forced me to look for plants today! And if we did not have this rain, these plants might not be as amazing to look at. Which made me think about how different my life would be if I never had those periods of "rain." How would my life be if everything just went perfectly all the time? Would I appreciate any of it? I don't think I would because even now, I struggle with keeping time at home to include God every day. It is because I can fill it with other things more easily again. When I think about this, it makes me sad. I am feeling incredibly determined to keep God a bigger part of my life than before the 2020 quarantine. I am trying to understand when I know that my life is so much better with

God as my focus, why is it that I do not just automatically do that? I guess because I am human. During the quarantine, it was so easy to do. I am still doing it, but it is a little bit more of a struggle because of the other things I am now able to do. And these are all very important things ... being with family and friends. But I pray I can keep it all in perspective and remember how important God was to me when it seemed so hopeless. When we were in a place of such uncertainty, I know I spent so much time with God trying to understand what was happening. And I feel I have learned so much. I will never regret having to slow down and be at home for a while. But then this afternoon, when I was just thinking it would never stop raining, the sun came out, and what a beautiful evening we had. Maybe today is like this Covid quarantine. We have been in a rainy period, and just when we think it will never stop, out comes the sun. I pray this will be the case. I don't want to lessen the severity of those this virus has touched. But there will be a better time again. And just like the sun today, it might just show up unexpectedly.

I am committing today to do my best to remain thankful especially for the "rain" in my life. Because I know I will be better for it and God will even send us a rainbow to remind us. To God be the glory!

~Image by Lorie

Where Are You Hiding?

As a kid, I loved playing hide and seek. Truth be told, I still liked to play it with my grandkids when they were younger. I love the orneriness that comes out when we played, me included! I like to watch the faith of a 1–2-year-old when they cover their eyes with their hands or a pair of glasses, believing no one can see them. And, of course, we, as adults, encourage them so we can hear them giggle and have fun. Then as 3-year-olds, they get some confidence and move to find a place (usually out in the open) and are so excited when we find them! They may use the same hiding place ten times in a row! But, as they get older, unfortunately, they can become good at it. Sometimes too good! I have already had to give in to some of the older ones because they became much more sly and secretive about their hiding. I was thinking about this when I was listening to a song today about God finding us. How many times have I tried to hide from God because I knew I was not really acting the way I should ... even if it was in a small way? Possibly I had the same downfall and then the same hiding place many times in a row! What a futile act for me to engage in. My grandkids may be able to outsmart me as they get older, but I will never be able to outsmart

God. No matter how sly or secretive I become. In fact, I learned a long time ago the harder I try to hide things from God, the more painful they are when they come to light. And yet, I have my human moments when I might think, oh, God did not notice that! Please tell me I'm not alone here!

It usually does not take long for me to realize I was wrong and confess. I guess when I think about hide and seek with God, if I am trying to hide from Him, he always seeks me out and finds me when I need it the most. We can count on that. And it is up to us how long the "game" will last. How long do we try to hide? Or do we just talk with God and be transparent? I mean, honestly, God has forever to wait on us. But when he "counts to ten" in any given situation, it's "ready or not, here He comes." He knows when we need Him to find us and will seek us out and never leave us alone, just because He cares that much about each one of us. What an amazing honor to know and trust this God of ours. To God be the glory.

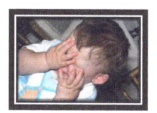

Lost And Found

Have you ever seen a picture that made you think of something that was lost? Marv took this picture of me taking a picture one day. When I saw it, I thought of the many years I spent taking pictures of people, weddings, etc. Of course, it was with a "real" camera! I honestly never thought I would be using a cell phone. But at any rate, this reminded me of what I had done for almost 30 years, only quitting because I needed a kidney transplant. And yes, there are days I miss it and wish I could do it again. But then I remind myself how grateful I truly am for God's leading. God has been so faithful in all the seasons of my life.

When I needed a job, He provided not just a job but a career I would love. And when I needed to focus on my kidney transplant, He provided a way for me to move forward and had Marv available to help me when needed. When I needed a kidney, He spoke to a dear friend's heart to make sure I would get a kidney. And her heart listened. Of course, having a transplant was not in my plans, but

God knew it would open new doors for me in other ways. So, have I lost some things and people through the years? Of course. I have lost dear parents. Sweet in-laws. And a very dear brother, brother-in-law, and sister-in-law to mention a few. But while those losses can be heartbreaking, I know God has a plan. I think about my parents and in-laws. The way the world is today would have been so overwhelming to them. And my dear brother and brother-in-law were in much pain. I know they must be relieved to no longer have that pain. I believe for this time in life, God knew they would all be better off with Him. So, while I look at this picture and my heart longs to be younger and still doing what I love, I need to take a step back and be grateful that God has a beautiful plan for my life right now also. And looking back at how faithful He has always been in my life only increases my faith in His plans for my future. And His plans are always better. Something lost, but much found. To God be the glory!

Dear Lord,

Thank you for being there for me so many times in my life. My faith has increased over the years because of Your faithfulness. Lord, if I feel a loss today, please remind me of the many, many blessings You have given me. I am so grateful for all You have done in my life and continue to do. Your love is unmatched by anyone. And for that, I am so thankful.

In Your Loving Name,

Amen

~Image by Marv

Winners Circle

It is said that people like to associate with winners. Which leads me to ask what makes a winner? Lots of money? Status? Popular? Of course, these are some of the human measurements of success or winning. Looking at this very human view, helps me understand why some people do not view God as a "winner."

God's view of winning is so different from ours. He sends His only son to earth to save us from our sins. Jesus was a lowly carpenter. He was not the most popular man on earth. Misunderstood. He had many trials to overcome. He died an extremely painful death while being spit at, called names, and ridiculed. He was never rich in dollar amounts.

He did not measure his worth by his bank account or his reputation in the community. Pretty much nothing we would look at today when trying to be a "winner."

So, the question remains... who is right? Humans? Does our worth, being considered a "winner," depend on how much money we have? Or our status in the community? Does it matter which political side we connect to? Or which "side of the tracks" we live on?

Or perhaps God is so much wiser than we could ever be. Rather than money, is kindness more important? Instead of status, should we have more humility? If our profession in life is not exciting or notable, should we be disgruntled or do the best job where God put us? Should our priorities be God, Family, and others? Or is the current trend to put ourselves first? "Me time." I deserve that. I am entitled to have this. But am I really?

I am putting it out there that I would venture to side with God. His wisdom is always perfect. And from what God has shown me in my life, He is a true winner! I am sticking with Him! To God be the glory!

~Image by Lorie

Choose God and you will always be in the winner's circle!

God Is Good

God is good. God is good. God is good. I heard someone say one time to repeat that over and over to let Satan know he cannot compare to what God can ever do for us. Going through a financial crisis in your life? "God is good." Are you going through relationship problems... even relationship catastrophes? "God is good." Are you struggling with things your kids are doing? The way they are choosing to live their lives. "God is good." Maybe you have lost a loved one. "God is good." Someone has deeply hurt you. Perhaps they have tarnished your name. Maybe they didn't repay you for the money they owed you. "God is good." Having health issues? "God is good. All the time." Financial stress? "All the time. God is good."

If we can believe that deep down in our hearts, there is nothing anyone can do to ever hurt us and nothing Satan can do to ever overcome the love God has for us. It took me many years to believe this. I was good at holding a grudge. I was excellent at remembering hurt. I have since learned it is not worth any of my time thinking about those things that can allow Satan to drag me down. Instead, I am choosing to remember "God is good. All the time. All the time. God is good." It is amazing how God honors that and offers us something Satan could never give us. A beautiful eternal life with God. What an amazing gift. To God be the glory!

~ Image by Lorie

Give Me Your Eyes

There is a song by Brandon Heath called "Give Me Your Eyes." I have always loved this song because it reminds me how easy it is to walk right beside people and have no idea how much they are hurting. I wonder how often I have looked right past someone whose heart was breaking. Who was hungry because they could not buy food? How many children have no real parents to love them and nurture them? And I had no idea, so I just kept walking.

Can you imagine if every time we crossed paths with someone, we could see into their life? We could see if they needed food. Needed clothes. Needed love. Needed an ear to hear them. Or just needed a smile. When I think of this, I get a bad feeling in the pit of my stomach. I know I cannot help everyone, and I'm sure that's why God has taken it upon himself to be the only one to see all the hurt. But He does allow a few people that need help to cross our path. The question is when God puts someone in our path, do we respond? I am sure I have failed at times with this. But I have tried to reach people when I am aware of someone hurting. God has put this heavy on my heart. I think because these days there are so many people who are hurting. Hurting financially. Emotionally. Relationships in trouble. Children not having parents around to show them how to live with purpose. It is a challenging time. If you feel this with me, let's try to reach out to someone today who we know needs it. If we each choose one, it will make a difference. If you are the one hurting, please allow someone to help. It is ok to ask for help. I am praying for a softer heart, much love to share, and for the eyes of Jesus to see those I would be able to help. To God be the glory!

~Image by Rachel Ryan

It is fun to watch how kids reach out to younger kids with acceptance. Another lesson that can be learned from children!

The Big Oak Tree

While driving "The Loop "in Flagler Beach, Florida, we came across this huge oak tree that had withstood all the hurricanes and storms for the past 500-600 years. (This is what they estimated it at.) It stood so tall and strong after all this time. I remember looking up at its massive limbs, like arms reaching out to cover me from anything that could hurt me. It was an awesome feeling. What is even more amazing is to realize that God has been here from the beginning, and His arms are stretched out so much wider to protect me every day of my life.

Now let me clarify that. It does not mean that God makes my life easy. Or that nothing hard will ever happen to me. Not at all. But it means He knows what is best for my life, so I can look forward to spending eternity with Him. And when things happen to me that seem overwhelming, I can envision His arms lifting me up and carrying me through. That is by far the most incredible feeling ever. As I stood under the massive oak tree, I imagined what it would look like if I could see God's arms around me. It is not something I can even fathom! What an amazing God we serve. I am thankful every day for those loving arms of God. To God be the glory.

Dear Lord,

Thank you so much for putting Your loving arms around me whenever I need them. You are faithful, and for that, I am so thankful. Lord, guide me today in all I do. And if something happens that is difficult today, I know I can count on Your arms wrapping around me so tight that I know it will be ok. Thank you for loving me so much, Lord.

In Your Loving Name,

Amen

~Image by Marv

Time with God

Do you ever have a day when there are so many things running through your head you are not sure which one to think about first? What I truly do not like is when I go through all that, and then it seems just too much to pick one…so I do none of them!!! Am I alone here?

I have had many ideas and things on my mind lately. And sorting them out myself just makes my head spin. Sometimes that is what stops me from writing! I cannot pick the words to write about. That's when I realize I have been too busy. When I was writing every day before, I never had to even think about what God wanted me to write about.

So, I am guessing I have been too busy to put those times with God first, and any "thoughts" worth writing about do not come to me without my time with Him. I hate admitting this, but without God, I am not a very good writer at all!!! But it also made me glad to realize that the thoughts I have written about in the past were truly God inspired. This has been a good wake-up call for me. Spending more time with God equals God speaking to me clearly. It does not mean God has left me. It means I have not been making Him a priority. And it really hit me when I tried to write, and no words came to me. So, this is my confession that God has not in any way, shape, or form left me… and I have not left Him. But I have not been spending the one-on-one time with Him that He so greatly deserves. And I plan to get back to putting Him first. I miss His words. His voice. And I know He misses mine. Put Him first, and His voice will come to you like a waterfall…loud and never-ending!

If any of you are feeling so busy that God gets moved down the priority ladder, I challenge you to join me and put Him first again! To God be the glory!!

~Image by Marv

God's Beauty

Chapter 5

God's beauty.

His forgiveness.

His love.

His grace.

His mercy.

His creation.

Let's bask in all of it.

~Image by Marv

Snowy Thoughts

SNOW ON MAY 8th? I had to ask God, what were you thinking? We seriously want to get outside and work. Plant flowers? Why bother when I need to keep covering them because it's so cold out! I must admit I felt a little peeved at God for this crazy little joke He was playing on us. But when I took the picture below, I was at my sister's house celebrating her birthday. I looked out the door, and this voice (my sister) said, "It sure is pretty!" She did it again... found beauty in something I was complaining about. But I realized that truly, as I wrote about before, "beauty is in the eye of the beholder." So why, when I look at something, do I choose to look at the problem? God reminds me in all sorts of ways that we have a choice. A choice to see beauty or ugly. Hope or fear. A choice to see solutions or problems. A choice to see good or bad. We can lay our worries on our minds or put them on God's shoulders. A choice to create discord or speak peace. We can choose joy or live in bitterness. I understand that we are all human, and sometimes we cannot seem to make the right choice every day. Believe me, I personally know this. But all God is asking of us is to at least honestly take the time to try to make the better choice and not just default to the negative. Remember, God forgives us when we fail, but He truly expects us to try. To God be the Glory!

~Image by Lorie

Do You Like the Wrapping?

Have you ever received a gift that was not what you had hoped for? At least it did not look like it by the wrapping. There is a story about a son with very wealthy parents who could give him anything he wished for except time and love. When he was ready to graduate, his father told him he was going to buy him the car of his choice. So as the day got closer, the son could hardly wait to get his new Ferrari. The graduation day came, and his father called him into his office and told him... here is your gift. It was a small rectangular box that would never hold a car! He opened the box, and inside was a Bible.

The son was so furious. He was promised a car! His father tried to talk to him, but he stormed out, never to return. As the years passed, his heart softened, and he decided to make things right with his father. So, he got in his car and headed for home. On his way home, he got a call saying his father had passed away. He was heartbroken. What had he done all these years? Why had he waited so long to talk to his dad? When the will was read, the father had left his son EVERYTHING. All his money, his mansion...everything. As the son was going through things in his dad's office, he looked up and saw the wrapped box his father had given him so many years ago.

He grabbed it from the shelf and accidentally dropped it. Inside was the Bible he had been so angry about. He noticed there was a Bible marker set in one place. He opened it and out fell a set of keys for a Ferrari. All those years ago, he never gave his father a chance to explain. He simply saw the wrapping and decided it was not anything he would ever want. The son ran to the garage, and there sat his car. The car he dreamed of. And suddenly, he realized what a horrible mistake he had made. But it was too late to apologize to his father.

How often do I do this? I ask God to help me with things that I want, but I expect God to give me exactly what I asked for, and it also had to be "wrapped" as I expected, or I was disappointed. For instance, about 30 years ago, I remember telling God that I wanted to be used for His glory. Well, He answered my prayers, but not in the "wrapping" I wanted. He had to take me through some tough times before I was truly ready to be used by Him at all! And as the years passed, I realized God knew exactly what He was doing. He knew the things in my heart that needed to change. Places in my life where I needed to grow. Was it in the "wrapping" I would choose? Not a chance. Did it wake me up to realize I needed to change? Absolutely! And God knew that. As soon as I realized He knew what was best for me, and I allowed Him to mold me the way He needed to, I felt such peace. God's still working on me, but He has given me so many "presents" (things I have asked for) that now I understand I simply needed to wait for His timing. I cannot always understand the "present" by the "wrapping." But He always knows the plan and just how to "wrap" it. To God be the glory!

4-Year-Old Wisdom

On any given day, when I pick my 4 year old grandson Noah up, he has to pick a dandelion for me. I just take it, smile, and say thank you Buster!! While I am honestly thinking, I'm not returning this weed to my house! I have so many already!! But, of course, he always checks to make sure I did not lose this precious little flower.

Then as we are driving down the road, Noah says, "Grandma, STOP! "I slowed down and said, "What is wrong, Noah?" He screams… "That man is mowing down all the dandelions!! We need to stop him!!!" Of course, at that point, I kept driving and tried to explain to him that we do that because dandelions are weeds and they will come right back. But that was not satisfying him. Pretty soon, he saw another person mowing the dandelions. He was so upset that someone would hurt, or worse, get rid of these precious flowers he picked for me. And in his 4-year-old wisdom, he made me think. Noah was able to see the simple beauty in a field of yellow flowers. Flowers that were weeds to me, but it was his way of showing his love to me in a way that he could. He did not consider them weeds. He did not want to see them get mowed down. He simply saw their beauty.

It was like God was saying to me, "Look at other people this way." Don't see them for their flaws. Or the burden they might be to us if we get too involved. See them for their beauty. God made dandelions to keep us in check about seeing beauty. They really do not hurt us. They really do not cause us any harm. The only disadvantage is to our minds when we choose to see the ugliness they cause when we want perfect carpet-like green yards. Will I still mow them? Yes. But I might feel a little bit of remorse because of this wise little 4-year-old!! So, the next time Noah gives me a dandelion. I am getting a very small vase to display in my kitchen. To show it the respect he feels it deserves! I really do not want Noah to stop seeing the beauty in things because of me! To God be the glory!

Beauty Is in My Eyes

Wow. What a beautiful evening! And Marv had off work today, so we got all our flowers planted. My knee is not so great... but the work got done. And now I can sit outside and enjoy the beauty of our labor!! The sun is shining. The birds are chirping, and the bullfrogs are making whatever sound they make! And I am appreciating how good life is right now. I was talking to a friend today and saying how much looking for the beauty around us can change our entire day. I can gripe and complain as well as anyone. And when I was looking at all the work that needed to be done, and my knee was hurting, I had a few not-so-good moments. But with the planting of every plant, the murmuring got to be a little less. Every pot that turned out just like I wanted it, and found its perfect place on the porch, made my complaining go away more. And I was reminded of how seeing the beauty of nature can profoundly change our attitudes. It can give us hope when there seems to be none. It can remind us of what an incredible creator we have. And how He created each one of us for a purpose. I know it may not always feel that way. But I know it is true. And when I am sitting here with a bad knee, or remember I had to have someone else's kidney put in me, if I just look around, I can still see so much beauty. I can sit in awe of so many incredible, amazing things. And when I hear the birds, I know they have a purpose. When I listen to the bullfrogs, I know they have a purpose. When I hear the dog barking off in the distance, I am sure he is making some family very happy. And yes, even this crazy old lady sitting on the porch with a bum knee still has a purpose. And I really need to realize that these might be some of my best times!

I know I say this often, but I had more peace in 2020 about many different things, and it was all during a strange time. And as I know, God does not care if He does things the way we think He should. He only cares that He does what is the absolute best thing for us.

So, does my knee hurt? Yes. Was I still able to appreciate this day? Absolutely! There are things that can make me feel sad or just not myself. But there is nothing that can ever steal my joy! And sitting out here on a night like tonight, I know in my heart that God is real. And He is amazing! And at this very moment, that is enough for me.

His creations like these baby birds on our property remind me of God's beauty and hope for the future. To God be the Glory!

~Image by Marv

Driftwood Beauty

Marv and I are absolute driftwood lovers. When we walk the beaches in Florida, occasionally we can find some, but our favorite place to get driftwood is Port Clinton, Ohio. I remember a time when we stayed in a Bed & Breakfast for our anniversary. We went to this beach where there is always a good amount of driftwood. We got out of our car, and there it was...a large piece of driftwood, just beautifully sitting there. I wanted that piece! Marv thought I was joking. But I was not. It was a huge statement piece. And while Marv was giving every logical reason we should not take it, this couple (my angels of the day) came up and started talking to us. They said they come every weekend and look for driftwood. He saw how badly I wanted that big piece and said to Marv, if you pull your car around, I'll help you load it. I am standing there saying, yes, yes! So, Marv got the car. They fit it in the car while Marv said, "I have no idea where you think you are going to put this!!" I just kept saying, I don't know either, but I'm sure there will be a time when we will be glad for it! We took it home, and I wondered what I could do with this. It lends itself to a base for a coffee table, but I just was not sure. Then guess who found a perfect place for it? Marv. We were doing some landscaping around our house, and he put it in the corner, and I loved it. Oddly enough, so did he. I put succulents in the crevices and thought to myself, what a gift I got that day at the beach. My angels came by and made sure I got it even if Marv was not crazy about it. I remember saying, have faith. We will be glad we got it. And then Marv produced the vision. It is interesting how we plan in our heads how something is going to go. When I first saw that piece, I was sure I wanted to make a coffee table, but Marv had the perfect vision for it. And I love it. Last weekend when we were in Port Clinton again, we found another smaller piece of driftwood to take home from that trip. And Marv came home and stuck it in a different bowl of succulents. Once again, I love it. Sometimes we can all wonder if we are paired with the right spouse. I think it is just human nature to question it. But I told Marv, more than once, I can see why God put us together. Because together we make one amazing person! God is good... all the time. All the time... God is good. To God be the glory.

~Images by Lorie

114

Let Freedom Ring

With all the things going on in our country these days and so many Facebook posts that make my heart hurt, I felt led to write something positive. I was thinking of freedoms that all of us as a divided country and, as currently free people have, we could hopefully agree that there are many things we have to be thankful for. Some may seem minor or even silly, but some countries do not have these freedoms. So here goes...

* The freedom of speech

* The freedom of religion

* The freedom to own whatever vehicle we want.

* The freedom to hop on a plane and

   go on a vacation.

* The freedom to drive to wherever we want.

* The freedom to sit and enjoy the sunshine.

* The freedom to disagree with people

   without fighting.

* The freedom to run to the store and

   pick up whatever we want.

* The freedom to own our homes.

* The freedom to own our own land.

* The freedom to be with our families and have fun.

* The freedom to own our own "stuff."

* The freedom to sit and listen to the

   birds without fear.

* The freedom to plant our own gardens.

* The freedom to write.

* The freedom to choose a career

   doing something we love.

* The freedom to choose God's forgiveness

   and love. And to live an eternal life with Him.

* The freedom to choose who we want

   to spend our lives loving.

* The freedom to have clean water to drink.

* The freedom to openly worship God.

There really are so many things in this country to be thankful for. And I do not ever want to take these little and big things for granted. I need to be thankful each day and pray these freedoms will never be snatched away from us. However, there is one freedom I mentioned that no one can ever take away from us…the freedom to choose God. What a blessing! I am challenging you to make your own list of freedoms for which you are grateful. And then do not take them for granted… ever again. To God be the glory!

~Image by Marv

Serenity

Marv and I absolutely love walking on the beach. Sitting on the beach listening to the waves. But for me, writing on the beach is my favorite thing to do. It is as if God simply talks to me through the ocean waves. For me, it's not all about the sun. It's about serenity. The peace that comes with the sound of the waves. The peace that comes from watching the birds on the beach. The peace and joy of watching sailboats let the wind catch them and guide them across the ocean. We like to go to beaches that are not swarming with people so that the serenity becomes very real. Sometimes there is not much sun. But there is much serenity and peace. And that is perfect as far as I am concerned. God is not only good, but He is also great. And watching the ocean waves, knowing just how far to go, proves that to me. To God be the Glory!

~Image by Lorie

The Swamp

This could sound like political writing, but it is not. I am not "draining the swamp." However, we did walk through a swamp yesterday. The Cypress swamp in the Highlands Hammock State Park in Florida. It was remarkably interesting, with so much natural beauty. So peaceful. So full of sounds of nature. So incredibly calming. We were a little disappointed we didn't see any alligators or crocodiles. But we saw some beautiful birds. It was so lovely to just stop and take it all in. We walked through once, just meandering to see what we could see. Then we walked it a second time, thinking we would walk faster for exercise, but new plants or little creatures caught our eyes that we had not seen the first time. It is so easy these days to not notice all there is in God's beautiful creation, but the beauty truly is in the eye of the beholder. In this swamp, there were many of the same plants and trees.

So, if you just walked through it without looking for the beauty, it would be quite easy to miss it. It is kind of like when we go through a "swamp" in our everyday life. It may seem overwhelming or just mundane. But if we choose to see the beauty God has put in front of us every day, no matter how hard it is to see or hear, we are better for it. I have found God often puts little "beauties" in my life when going through a tough time. Even though I must look a little harder sometimes, it is always worth it. I had gone through some negative years in my life until I figured this out. So, if you are going through a "swamp" right now in your life, I would encourage you to look for the beauty in it...no matter how hard it is to find. Trust me, you will be a better person for it. We just need to look and listen for His mighty creativity in this beautiful world He has given us. To God be the Glory!

Dear Lord,

You are the mighty and creative maker of this world. I praise You for the beautiful things You have put in this world for us to enjoy. Today I am praying for those out there who are going through a "swamp" right now in their life. Please help them stop, look, and listen for the "beauties" You still put in their life, even amongst the mundane daily troubles. Help me to focus today on the good things in my life rather than the frustrations.

In Your Sweet Name,

Amen

~Images by Marv

Hugs and Hanging Out

Every time when our grandkids were younger and I would go to their house, they would run up to me, Grandma, Grandma, "I go your house?" Sometimes I had to say no for several reasons. But recently, I got to spend time one day with our 2-year-old grandchild, Noah. He just kept saying in the car, "I go your house, Grandma!" And he even knew when to turn to get to my house! While he was eating lunch, I started walking away from him, and he said, "Wait, Grandma, wait. "I said, what, Noah? He said before you go, I give you a hug. Well, he melted my heart. It was 2020, and social distancing went out the door. If I am going to take a chance of becoming sick, it will be with my grandkids! He gave me a big old hug as he gently rubbed my back. I almost started crying.

What is it about a two-year-old hug, or any grandchild's hug for that matter, which can bring tears to your eyes? The reason is, at that exact moment, it truly hit me how blessed I am. We played with blocks. We made a road with blocks showing how to get from his house to my house. We built towers. We raced cars. We ate mac n cheese. We cuddled under a blanket and read books. We watched "Super Why." We decorated the living room with marbles. And we cleaned the infamous "train" all the grandkids drove around. We just basically spent time together. And that was all he needed. And that was exactly what I needed. It was a wonderful day. I hope I can always be as happy about the simple things as a two-year-old. Another affirmation why Jesus said to the children, "Come." And why God does not want us to turn children away. We could learn a lot about life from them! I know hugs & hanging out are the best. And I found so much beauty in that. To God be the glory!

~Image by Lorie

Beauty of the Seasons

As I was driving today, I noticed the beautiful clouds!! And I thought, what a great mix of summer and fall! Blue skies and autumn clouds! What a beautiful sight! That felt so right today, being it is the last day of summer. I was thinking of this past summer and what a wonderful time it has been. There have been struggles. But as always, God walked through them with us.

Marv and I built a backyard deck and fence completely by ourselves. And still stayed married to celebrate our 45th anniversary! We saw many grandkids ball games. Enjoyed the beautiful weather. I enjoyed seeing my grandkids two days a week all summer.

We went on a trip to Florida with Alex, Brooke, and their family. Went to COSI with Abby and her kids. Adrienne came home from Florida, and I got a complete family picture. I must admit, it always bugged me. For almost 30 years, I photographed families and helped them pick out the best images. So, out of all the people in the world, it felt odd that I had not had one for over 10 years!! But now I was blessed to get one!

Overall, we had a busy, beautiful, fulfilling, and amazing summer. Autumn has always been my favorite time of year. So, these clouds were a mix of a fantastic summer and the beautiful fall colors to come. The best of both seasons! I am grateful for all of it!! Thank you, Lord, for reminding today of the incredible beauty You have put in front of us to enjoy. I am looking forward to the amazing colors you will paint this coming autumn! To God be the Glory!

~Image by Marv

Who's Your Head Honcho?

Marv is a good dad. A good papa. And loved so much by all of us. I am so blessed to have him as the papa to my grandma! I like to think of Marv as our head honcho. He is at the top of our totem pole and deserves to be respected because of that. We are a family who enjoys having fun, poking fun, laughing, and then laughing some more. We are very blessed. Marv comes to my rescue all the time. I know if I really need him, he will be there. But I was thinking, while Marv is the head of our family, who is the head of my life? Who takes care of me when no one else can? Who watches over me every second of every day? Who works literal miracles just when I need them? While Marv is great, he is still human. I feel so blessed to have a God who is willing to come to my rescue when no one else can. Someone who can love me no matter how much I mess up. Someone who gives me so much purpose in my life.

So, I guess you could say God is the ultimate head honcho of my life. I cannot imagine living life any other way. My prayer today is that if you are reading this and you do not have God as the leader of your life, this will be the day He speaks to your heart, and you will be open to hearing His voice. Allow Him to be your ultimate friend, teacher, builder, helper, and leader of your life. Because I can testify to the fact there is no better way to live! To God be the Glory!

~Images by Lorie

What a Difference a Year Makes

I am sitting out by the ocean today, just soaking in God's beauty and wonder amidst all the pain in this world. 2022 has been an unusual year so far for us (and many people). Different kinds of pain, sorrow, disappointment, and tests on our faith. There is a song that says, "Joy comes, tears fall. I've learned that there is beauty in it all," and it says, "God is good." I am thinking about this right now. Last year I would have to say Marv and I had the most beautiful vacation we have ever had. It was full of old and new friends. We went many miles seeing many things we hadn't seen before. Enjoying the absolute beauty of it all. Really not one day where we had any trouble to speak of. Going into this year, we anticipated the same thing, if not better. But we soon realized God had other plans.

There was much pain, fear, and disappointment in the first 6 weeks of our 2022 journey. Marv had Covid and was in the hospital for 14 days. I was not able to see him. But as we look back on it, we cannot believe all that God had planned for us. Family and friends showed up in so many ways. There are too many "God moments" to put in one of my "thoughts." Marv and I feel truly blessed and cared for. We may not have had all the adventures we had last year. We may not have felt good a lot of the time. We may still struggle with being too tired to do things we had hoped to do. But in amongst the "tears falling," there has also been much "joy in it all." We are thankful. We feel blessed. We are together. And we have once again been reminded how God looks out for us. It is often through people around us like family and dear friends. God is such an incredible Father. And His love for us is unending. My heart goes out to those that are hurting today. I pray that no matter the circumstances, you can find peace. Especially in this crazy world we are living in. God is bigger than any of this…even if we cannot see it right now. And God is certainly good! To God be the glory!

Happy to be back on the beach!

Doing God's Will

Chapter 6

Only when we desire God's

will for our life, can we

have true peace.

~Image by Marv

Gifts from God

I know God gives each of us gifts and talents. I have often wondered exactly what my skills are. I'm sure we all have wondered about this at some point in our lives. Even if we don't feel like ours are obvious talents, sometimes it can just be the talent of being kind. That is a big one these days. The gift of praying. It may not always be obvious, but sometimes those are the most important. We have a 9-year-old grandson with a gift for listening to and playing music. I have encouraged him to play piano since he was 4 months old. This kid amazes me every time I am around him. He sits down and plays the piano just by listening to songs or even creating his own "songs." Or sometimes, he will just put his own twist on something he has heard before. He will sit and play it until he gets it down the way he wants it. One day he created a song that was so beautiful, but he did not want me to video him because He needed a "third" hand (me) for this song. So, I sat down beside him, and he showed me the chords to play on the lower register. I played them as he played his new song. It sounded incredible. His God-given talent blows my mind. You know us grandmas, I just want to encourage him to use this amazing talent God has given him. I pray that he will someday choose to use his gifts for God's glory. I know there will be trying years between now and then, but I believe he will get there someday.

We also have a 9 yr. old granddaughter that can cook and bake just about anything. She is amazing and I pray she will also use this one of her many God -given talents. Trust me, she already has! She even baked cupcakes for a fund raiser at her church! I cannot wait to see what our other grandkids will do!

Today I just want to encourage each of us to use our God-given talents. No matter how insignificant we may think they are. Because God has given each of us gifts that He chose for us. And it puts a smile on God's face when we are willing to use them for His good. To God be the glory!

God Like

I have not felt coordinated with God lately. Not very "God like." Has anyone else ever felt like that? You go to do something you can normally do on any day, and you cannot do it. For me, it was writing. I was talking to a friend today, and I was telling her I just have not had the words to say. I knew I needed to keep waiting until my heart was clear. I was afraid of what my fingers would type. And she commented... that was wise. It would not have been from God. That is when it hit me. Yes. That is why I have not been able to write. Because when I write, I want it to be uplifting and God knew it would not be positive because of how I was feeling. I also want it to be honest and from my heart. It would not have been a blessing to anyone if I had forced the writings.

He was protecting me from writing things I would regret. And for that, I am thankful. I have had various things happen. I have gotten a little frustrated with the hateful words on social media. I have been far too busy. And my heart has not been where it should be. I have prayed and talked to God about this. I have asked for forgiveness, and I know He has forgiven me. He confirmed it for me by allowing me to want to share again. I find it interesting that no matter how much we know about right and wrong, we can still stray from what is right ...we are human. I am so grateful that God understands our weaknesses and not only puts up with them but watches over us while we go through our mistakes. And not only does He walk with us and watch over us, but He also guides us to the right place again and restores our peace. He is an amazing and faithful friend and leader. To God be the Glory!

~Image by Lorie

God Moments

Prayers answered! There have been several prayer requests that we have been praying for recently that have been answered. I cannot share details, but I am praising God this morning for all He does for us! And I can share some of the many past God moments in my life.

There was a time in our life when I wasn't sure how we would be able to feed our kids. We were going through multiple trials all at the same time. I am sure there are some out there who know what I'm talking about. The phrase... "When it rains, it pours" was my motto for years. It was one thing after another. But I want to share one of the many miracles God showed me during these times. At one point in time, there was a bill I was struggling to pay. The remaining balance on it was approximately $300. I remember praying about it, but my faith was more like the size of a mustard seed during that period of my life. This is when I realized God means what he says in his Word. Because my little faith was enough to produce an incredible "God Moment." One day I came home and found an envelope with $300 in it in my door handle. I about dropped to my knees. I had not told anyone about this. Only Marv, me, and God knew we needed this. And yet, the cash was inside an envelope with these words handwritten on the front, "God put you on my heart today." And the exact amount we needed! These moments in our lives are acts of kindness from people who are open to God's voice and follow it. But I give God the ultimate praise for talking directly to their heart. And I am so thankful their heart was open to it. This is not the only time this has happened to us. There was another similar instance also. I will never forget these many miracles God has shown me over the years. And He deserves glory. So, To God be the Glory!! I am praying today for miracles in the lives of those people who need them! Not only financial ones but health and relational issues. Lord, by your miracles, increase their faith in You. I am also praying if God touches our hearts to reach out to someone, our hearts will be open! To God be the Glory! God will not leave us to drown if we have faith, He can help us!

~Image by Marv

The Art of Saying No

When I think of God's house, I think of my church. Or any church. I think about the time that is spent taking precious care of those buildings out of reverence to God. We want to make sure that we are responsible and take care of our church because when we gather there, we can feel God's presence. And that is a good thing.

But today, I want to think about God living in me. Thinking about how my body also becomes God's house. I had a very rough time in March - October one year. I had no energy. I laid around more than I should have. And at some points, I felt like...why is God doing this to me? I want to be used by Him. But I can't help it when I feel like this.

I sometimes prayed that God would give me the strength to get through the day. Then it hit me hard one day that God is not doing this to me. I was not getting the right kind of or enough sleep. I was committing to a lot of things without really knowing if they were things God wanted me to do. Nothing bad...just too many! I was convinced God wanted me to say yes to everything anybody asked me to help with. Bad thought!

I think after praying and whining for months, God put it right in my face. If I wanted to feel better, I also had a part that I am responsible for doing. God is not going to magically make me feel better and give me more energy when I'm not allowing myself to rest and recover when I need to. I am not saying He couldn't do that as a miracle for me. But He also needs to know I am willing to do the things I need to do to take care of my body. Part of that is learning the art of saying...NO. It is amazing how God can work in us when we are willing to care about what HE asks of us to do, not everyone else around us.

If my body is God's house, I need to take care of it out of respect for Him. And yes, just as when I enter a church, I can feel His presence in me. And if I am worn out. Tired. Constantly hurting, God cannot use me in the way He wants to. So, when I try to take care of myself, it is because I am taking care of God's house, so I feel good enough for Him to work through me. I had to have a kidney transplant. There was nothing I could do about that. It was not because I was diabetic or had high blood pressure. For me, it was something that just happened because of certain past doctors not dealing with issues I was having. So, God understands when I need to rest. He understands when I need to say no.

God expects me to only commit to those things He is asking me to do. Those I will be able to handle. All the other stuff that keeps me from doing God's will for my life is not necessary, and God really expects me to seek His leading in what I do. And then be ok with saying no when it is not His will for my life.

So, I will admit that saying no does not come naturally to me. But I have decided that if I will disappoint God if I always say yes to everything, then I need to learn how to say no. So, this is another New Year's resolution of sorts. I want to master the art of saying no so I can be rested and feel good enough to be useable by God. To God be the Glory!

Dear Lord,

I come to you today knowing that I have not always done the things to take care of my body that you have expected of me. I am asking forgiveness for this. And asking you will give me the resolve to do the day-to-day things I need to do and to learn how to gracefully say no, so I can be available to You. Thank you for living in me and for your forgiveness. You are an amazing God, and You are worthy of me taking care of your home in me.

In Your Holy Name,

Amen

~Image by Marv

Being Productive

I was thinking about how productive my last two days have been. I was able to get so many things done. You might be thinking, it is kind of odd for me to be so amazed and feel like... "Wow! I got so much done!!" But I do feel like that. Not every day is a task-oriented productive day for me. Not every day is a sunny, "wow" kind of day. But the last two days were. The first thing I did was turn on my Christian music. It seems when I am playing that uplifting music in the background, I am more "productive." I prayed for the people on my "prayer wall" and made some meals for us and some for friends who needed them.

I got my huge mess cleaned up from cooking. (This is a chore because I do not have a dishwasher and am a messy cook!) I was able to get my raised garden planted that Marv made for me. I watered all the flowers and plants on the property, which takes a long time because we have a lot! I accomplished some writing that I had been wanting to work on. I was able to communicate with a few friends, which always makes for a good day. I ran some much-needed errands. Why am I telling you everything I did the last two days? I have to admit I kind of snickered when I would see on Facebook that someone posted they changed their sons diaper! Doesn't that go without saying? So, you could be snickering at me and saying, why do I care she made meals or planted her garden, ran some errands, or did some writing? I certainly do not want to come across like I think every little thing I do in a day is very important to you! But I do have a purpose for writing this. Sometimes we need to sit down and think about the things we do in a day. And what is it that makes us feel "accomplished"? There are days I will not get as many physical things done, but I might get more writing done. And vice versa.

But when I really think about it, if I wake up, I pray to my creator with a grateful heart, honor God in what I do, and do one thing that will make God say, well done, then it is a fantastic day. Because in the end, that is what will truly matter. I am so used to thinking I feel accomplished if there were a lot of physical chores I could check off my list. But I know in my heart God is not judging me by how many tasks I got done. He is just longing for my attention and for my time well spent with Him on His behalf. So, I am challenging myself at the end of the day to look at what I "accomplished" the same way God would look at it. Did I spend time with Him? Did I honor Him? Did I share His love with someone who really needed it? Did I listen to His voice to guide me through the day? When I look at that list of what God considers "accomplished," I do not see anything about projects, making money, cleaning my house, running errands, laundry, or dishes! The matters of the heart, love for others, and letting others know of our amazing God is on God's list. So, on days when I cannot get "things" done, it can still be a great day I just do what God would have me do.

If I do not have the energy to do a lot of physical things, can I still pray for someone? Can I send someone a word of encouragement or hope? Can I spend time talking with God? Can I spend time in His Word? I am saying that God gives us all kinds of days. Sometimes we have energy, and we can check a lot off our lists. Some days we can't. But either way, we can feel accomplished if we look at it like God would. And if you are in a situation where you do not always want to conquer the world, then just reach out to one person that day and give them hope. Show them God's love in some way. I guarantee God will still say. "Well done," even if our list has not gotten any shorter. Because things we see as task-oriented accomplishments are not always the kind of accomplishments that God sees. I try to remember God's version of a good day can be quite different from the world's ideas. So, I am praying that God will continue to work on my heart and put people in my path who need hope so I can help. And when I do not have the energy to be planting, painting, cleaning or even going anywhere, I can still be useful in God's eyes. He asks us to have faith and pray. These are the most important "tasks" that will ever be put on my list! To God be the Glory!

~Image by Lorie

Bearing Fruit

Today I saw something I never knew existed. A palm tree that bears fruit!! It was beautiful. Wispy leaves with oranges hanging from them. So unique. I found out it is called a Jelly Palm.

This palm tree made me think about how different and unique we must seem when we bear fruit for God. It is something beautiful, plus these days it can also cause us to look unique.

God wants us to be a light. Be beautiful to others around us. Make others ask…what is so different about that person? To look the way God intended us to be. Why is that person bearing fruit? Why do they have such joy?

I am feeling so blessed today that God has walked with us through yet another dark time while Marv was in the hospital with Covid. And once again, God was faithful.

So, it is important for me to bear fruit for Him. And this palm tree is a reminder to me that I may look different. I may feel like an outsider sometimes because of my beliefs, but that's not only OK, t it is also how God wants me to be.

That does not mean things will be perfect or that I am perfect, far from it. But I want to make sure I am doing my best to give God the glory for His continual faithfulness and love He shows us. And I am learning every day how to do things that will bear fruit for God. To God be the glory!

~Image by Lorie

Who's Your Rock?

It is an interesting question. Sometimes we look for our rock to be with family or friends. And unfortunately, that does not always turn out well. While most family and friends want to be there for you, they can only be a stepping stone in a path God has planned for you. And stepping from one "stone" to the next with grace while trusting God can be one way for God to increase our faith. And it really can increase our faith if we let God be our rock and allow him to use those around us to be the stepping stones. I have found we as humans, are just that...human. There is a limit to what we can do, and God may need to use a whole trail of stepping stones to get to the place He has planned for us. But we must allow those people to help us. And it may not all be family. It may not even be all people we know.

Sometimes God will plant a much unexpected "stone" in our path along the way. It could be someone you randomly meet in a store that has been down a similar path as you and gives encouragement. It may be a random meeting when you are standing at a gas pump waiting for your tank to fill. God may speak to someone's heart just at the right time, and they respond to His voice. They have no idea why they are to speak to you... but God knows. And He will direct those people to you. He does things that seem so very random to us, but He knows exactly what He is doing. He knows when we need certain things and people in our life, and He will provide...if we allow Him to. I could write a book on those times in my life! God is good. God is faithful. God is kind. God cares about us. And He knows what is best for us. Not necessarily what is easy for us, but what is best. And if you accept those "stones" He puts in front of you, your path will lead you right to God, the true rock. To God be the glory.

~Image by Marv

Your Lunchbox

I heard a preacher once talking about what we put in our kid's "lunchbox." I just had to share these thoughts while they were fresh in my mind. Some are thoughts he had, but most are my own. Either way, they are worth sharing. When we pack lunch for our kids, we usually try to pack stuff that is good for them. Things to make them healthy and be able to feel good so they can manage the day. So why is it that when our kids are young, and still at the age we can shape them, we aren't as careful about filling their "spiritual lunchbox"? That means filling their heart with things that can keep them spiritually healthy and ready to face each day. Mostly for when they are older, and not having us parents there to tell them.

I am as guilty as the next person. It is so easy to get wrapped up in the things the world thinks are important to do, such as sports, music, schoolwork, etc. All these things are great, and some are necessary. But sometimes, we let the things God thinks are important go by the wayside. Perhaps because the people around us are right here and will notice if we are not allowing our kids to become "successful." Somehow because God is not physically here beside us, we think He won't notice if we let spiritual things slide. That is something the 2020 quarantine did for me. Helped me remember what is important to God. I was never that wise when my kids were growing up. I just wanted the best for them. It is a natural human motherly feeling to want to shelter them from everything. To make sure they do not get hurt. Or they do not make mistakes. Especially if their mistakes might embarrass us in front of other, more "perfect" parents. I have come to realize through the years that all God really wants us to do, is help our kids to know God. And then give them the free will to choose to believe or not. No matter the mistakes they may make. We cannot make good choices for them. We can only guide them. If we think about it, isn't that what our Heavenly Father does for us? He made clear the difference between right and wrong. Then He put that conviction in our hearts and let us choose what to do. And I do not know about you, but I made plenty of mistakes. And they all taught me so much, which has shaped me into who I am today. And I am sure I'm not done making mistakes and learning! But I do wonder how many times God was "embarrassed" by my horrible choices. But he still loved me, no matter what. I think of my own kids. There were times I wanted to crawl under my bed for a few years until the embarrassment of choices they made settled. But I still loved them, no matter what! And I always will. I think I am trying to say that we tend to make parenting hard. We read books by well-meaning physiologists on how to be the perfect parent. When all God asks us to do is love unconditionally as He does with us, discipline when necessary, and teach them about Him. We must accept mistakes will be made, by both them and us! But we need to always love them anyway. Because each one of us must make our own choices. And there will come a time when we cannot make choices for our kids anymore. I honestly believe if we teach our kids that God is important, even if they make some bad choices along the way, they will eventually repent and come back to what they know in their hearts is right, and God will forgive them as should I. I am not promoting letting your kids run wild. Just saying I have found that I can trust my family with God through prayer more than anything I could ever tell them. It was just in my heart to share this with you. I am hoping it will speak to someone out there. To God be the Glory!

 I will always love you this much!!

Kindness Matters

Chapter 7

I tell my grandkids,

"Kindness Matters,"

which means I need to live by

those words also!

~Image by Lorie

Fence Thoughts

I have written before about clinging to the "vine" when going through rough times. And I mentioned that I thought God must have put a fence up around me for protection, so I could hang on. Today I was thinking that for me, my "fence" is Marv, my family, and my friends when I went through tough times, God used them to help me. All in their own unique ways. I got physical help, listening ears, prayer, and Marv stuck by me and did whatever was needed. This made me think about people who do not have family or a support system around them. How difficult that must be to hang on. Sometimes we just need that human touch or voice or even someone bringing us a meal or saying a prayer for us. It saddens me when I think about people who do not have that.

God put on my heart today to say to any of you reading this, if you are going through a rough time and just need a listening ear, you can always talk to God if you do not have anyone close to you. He is the best! Knowing God, I am sure He will put someone in your path to become that person you need to help hang on. Sometimes talking to someone else allows God to work through that person to help solve a problem. And often in a way you could never imagine!! I have had that happen so many times in my life. God can work in weird ways. And sometimes, He just needs people to help Him conduct His miracles. These are trying times, and much bitterness and anger out there. I have my views. You all have yours. And that is ok. God has it all in his hands. Today I pray for God to bring someone who has a listening ear and a praying heart into your life. I have been through many trying times myself. Do not ever be embarrassed to seek help when you need it. God does his best work through trials and kind people. It does not matter if those people are family, old friends, or even new friends God put in your life. I pray the boards in your fence will become long and strong and you will never walk alone again! To God be the glory!

~Image by Lorie

Worship or Waste?

I have been burdened lately with how to worship God. What is appropriate? Do we need to be quiet to be respectful? Or should we clap our hands and stretch them up to praise God. I have struggled with this little detail. I am more of the kind of person who wants to raise my hands to praise God with all I have. But I grew up in a church believing quiet was more reverent. I was thinking about how Mary knelt at Jesus's feet and poured out all her perfume, which was equivalent to a year's wages. When she did this, Judas said, "What is all this waste for?" Jesus stopped him and said, "This is not a waste; she is worshipping with all she has." Judas, like many of us, thought it was a waste for her to give all the perfume she had. He could understand putting some on His feet, but ALL OF IT? Judas believed that it was not wise to waste perfume. Why not be prudent and keep some for later? Mary had a kind heart and was just showing God her love extravagantly. If anyone deserves that, wouldn't it be Jesus? I thought about my own life. Do I give God ALL I can...whether it be how I worship, my time and energy, my resources, or stretching my life to help someone in need? Or do I simply do the minimum I can get away with? I doubt I would be alone if I said that many times I have only given or done the absolute minimum I could. But today, I am challenging myself to do more. Be more. Give it all to God. My entire family, time, money, worship...everything. He deserves it. God gave His only son to save me (and you too if you choose Him). Jesus went through so much for us to have complete forgiveness. He gave it all. When I remember this, why would I settle for a partial commitment in return to Him? He deserves more. So, when giving your all to worship and praise to God, do not hold back. Let God see you give everything! To God be the Glory.

~Image by Diane

S.O.U.L. Singers praising God!!

Another Day... Another Blessing

As I was waking up this morning, I was trying to decide how to start my day. I am not a morning person anymore. When I had the studio and was raising kids, I was a night owl and a morning person out of necessity. Now I find myself enjoying strictly being a night owl.

So, the question is... what will make me get up and get going? Should I wake up and think of all the things to do today? Immediately start on my list, so I feel accomplished. Or wake up and have my caffeine of choice to boost my body? Perhaps I should just sleep a little longer...then I wouldn't be so tired? Or I could do what I know works best. Hang out with God first. I could spend time in prayer. Bringing my concerns to him. My thanksgiving. And listening to His will for me today. Do I do this every morning? If I am honest, no. But I certainly try to because I have found that my day goes smoother when I do. And that does not mean it will be all peaches and cream. It means I can feel God's presence and peace to manage whatever comes my way that day. And that is enough for me.

What a blessing that is. And Lord, please help me to want to get out from under those cozy blankets! To God be the glory!

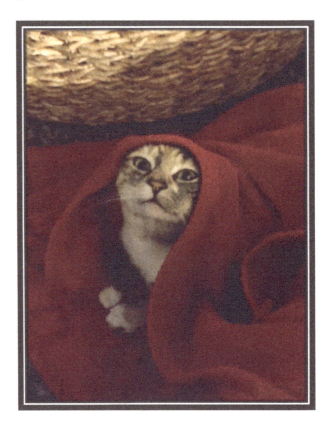

~ Image by Adrienne

Our Past

Our daughter Adrienne was sorting through some things today and sent me this photo she found of her and her grandparents at her high school graduation. As I looked at it, I thought about how fast this time has gone. And how things have changed so much. I doubt I am the only one that thought I had so much more time when I was younger! Now I wonder where it went. I remember hearing "old" people say that and thinking, that is crazy! So, I guess I am either just old now, or maybe more mature, but I can understand how precious time is with my family. And it also makes me feel good about all those years when you could not just raise your cell phone and take a good picture, that we were able to record many memories for people. I never really thought about that until I saw a picture like she sent me today. It was not a spectacularly composed picture. I do not even know who took it. But we will never have another picture like this. My mom and Marv's mom and dad have all passed away. How glad am I that someone took this? Extremely. It reminds me of good times in the past. And I am so grateful to that person who gave us this gift to remember. As I was thinking about photographs and how I stumbled upon a career in photography, I realized I did not stumble at all. I was led to do that. It could be nothing else. I went through some amazing times and some really challenging times, but I learned so much through it all. And I am not even talking about learning how to use a camera! I am referring to so many things that have led me to where I am now. Do I wish some of those things had never happened? Yes. I do. Am I grateful that all of it led me to my understanding of God's grace and forgiveness? Absolutely. I am so grateful for the way God leads us when we do not even understand what He is doing. One prayer changed my entire life. A prayer from my heart to use me for His glory. And he showed me how I had to change and taught me in many ways how to do that. I am not saying I have arrived. Not at all. But I know He has not given up on me yet. He is such a kind God who gently holds our hands through this journey of life. And, for that, I am profoundly grateful. To God be the glory!

Forgetful Thoughts

Ok, I am sure I'm not alone on this... so please be honest when you ask yourself the question, could this be me?

Today is one of my dear friends' birthdays. We do not see each other very often, but we still think of one another and keep in touch periodically. I texted her yesterday to say happy birthday because I thought of it and knew if I waited, it would slip my mind, and I would once again totally miss it. I called her and shared what I had done. She understood exactly what I was saying, as I knew she would. This morning I opened my devotional, and there was her name! At one point, when I was in an organized state of mind, I wrote it in my devotional book on this day so I would remember.

So, to be clear, here is a recap. I called my friend a day early to wish her a happy birthday, so I would not forget to do it today. Then I totally forgot I wrote her name in my devotional book so I would remember to tell her today. I could do nothing but laugh...and text my friend back so we could both laugh! Some days I wonder how I worked the number of hours I did when our kids were growing up, was always involved in their school activities, and kept everything straight!! I decided God knew what he was doing when he determined the age range for us to have kids! As I read my devotional, it talked about how God most often calls on those of us who feel inadequate to do what He calls us to do. How appropriate on a day like today! It spoke of wanting to help people when you see someone who needs it. I have been in those situations before and felt inadequate. But God led me through doing what He needed from me. Sometimes I have wondered if what I did was the right thing or even enough. But then I realized I did what God asked of me, and that is all I can do. I may never see the results of that situation, and I am ok with that because I know God will remember to do what is needed next.

Why am I connecting these things? First, because it was in my devotional this morning. Next, not always remembering things can make me feel inadequate. And yet God still chooses to ask me to reach out to others that He puts in my path. And that helps me be ok with where I am in my life. The point is… we are all usable in some way. And if we allow God to, He will continue to use us. My mom could not get around the last number of years in her life. But she could pray. I still have a couple of her prayer lists. She often thought she was not useful anymore. I remember reminding her that those prayers were why she was still here! So… today, I know there is one thing I will never forget. If God asks me to respond to something He sets in front of me, He thinks I am still worth using. And when I laugh at my total "age of mind," it is so good to remember that God has me (and you!) here for a reason. And if I can hear the reason, I will respond. Because if God thinks I am still worth it, then I am. Thank you, God, for that! Let's be kind to those of us who don't always remember everything. Someday it could be you!!To God be the glory!

~Image by Lorie

Choose Joy

Chapter 8

I don't know about you,

but sometimes, I just have to choose joy

and not let anyone or anything

steal it from me.

And I also must make sure I don't steal my joy

with my own attitude!

~Image by Brooke

Being Thankful

I was feeling a porch thought again today because Marv shared with me some pictures he took from our porch and around the property. I had to admit some came in a close second to our beach pictures. I mean, well... they were very pretty. Nothing can beat a good ocean picture. But looking at these images just spoke to me about the beauty all around us. And I am, just for a few days, challenging myself to find beauty where I am. I know it is easy to say that we are thankful, but have you ever sat and made a list? I was thinking. We have the most beautiful sunrises and sunsets from our porch. There are no trees, so we have a perfect view. Marv has captured some magnificent moon pictures off our porch. There is beauty in all seasons, even winter! So here is my list of some of the things I am thankful for just from the view of my porch:

1) The sunrises (everywhere, not just at the ocean)

2) The sunsets (everywhere)

3) The many moons that God displays for us

4) The snow over the pond

5) Something on my porch I am grateful for is what I call the "door table" that Marv made for me and surprised me with! I love decorating it every season.

6) I am grateful for such a peaceful view from our porch any time of the day!

7) I am grateful for our porch furniture I can sit on to write, or that Marv and I can relax on. (But not like old people!)

I am throwing out a challenge today for everyone to sit and make a list of things you can be thankful for just from where you are sitting. It is amazing what you can find. To God be the glory!

~Images by Marv

Choosing Joy

A few years ago, I wrote some "porch thoughts." About how peaceful it was to sit on our front porch and look around and be grateful for all God has given us. I also posted a challenge on Facebook to sit still for a 49-second video I made, to hear all the beautiful sounds in such a gorgeous, peaceful place. I felt blessed to be here. Now a few years later, we are still here. But it can be a challenging place to be these days. There is a historical barn being reconstructed close to us. It will be good in the end. But getting there has been a challenge. Especially when living here!! I have had days of frustration.

Days of not wanting to go outside…so I did not have to look at it. Days of being tired trying to keep up with all the mud. And then it hit me! I took another 49-second video of the same area as before. Previously it was green grass. A beautiful pond. Birds singing. The sound of bullfrogs. Total peace and beauty. But when I took the new video, I realized that even if there is now a Port-a-John in my view when I walk out the door, mud everywhere, equipment, and nails in the driveway, I could still hear the birds, the bullfrogs. The wind chimes, making music. And that brought me peace. It reminded me that even when things are challenging around us, God is still present. He is still here for me. We just need to trust him and enjoy the many blessings he has given us! So… am I human? Yes. I still get frustrated some days. But I am trying to look for the blessings all around us. And remember that God is still here, and it will all be good in the end. And the things I see around me are not where my joy comes from! It comes from Jesus living inside my heart. I need to remember no matter what changes, God is still here with me. I challenge all of us to remember this today; there is nothing that can steal my joy unless I allow it to. Not even a Port-a-John!! So…today, I choose joy. And I am still grateful to be here in this place. To God be the glory!!

Crazy Day Thoughts

It was another beautiful day in Ohio. I am feeling blessed. The weather reminded me of when we were in Florida! We took a walk in the park, spent time just sitting on our front porch, then had a peaceful fire and roasted hotdogs. The sky was magnificent until it wasn't! Suddenly the sky went dark, and the wind was whirling like a small twister. Now understand, where we live, we are very used to high winds. Often our porch furniture will be pushed right up against our rail. But tonight, we saw something we had never seen before. We ran outside to move our furniture, and the wind was swirling with such force we could hardly walk. Suddenly, the wind took my large porch rug and pulled it out from under the coffee table. Then, while the wind was pushing the table toward the rail, the rug was picked up, and started flying like a magic carpet! Up over the rail and into the yard. I thought I was going to lose my rug! Not to mention all three chairs were being thrown about. I said to Marv, it's like a tornado! And yet, I still tried to go after my inexpensive rug!! As if it had blown away, it could not be replaced. But I guess at that moment, my rug just seemed too important! The most amazing thing was, when I cried tornado, Marv said, I think it really could be! For those of you who do not know my husband, he is generally such a calm man that I can get aggravated. He thinks I get excited enough for the both of us. Such an annoying yet sensible trait for him to have. So, when he agreed with me, I was in awe. Almost like I had forgotten our current situation. Perhaps I wasn't overreacting? Hmmm. That was interesting! It made my day. Until I thought about the reason that he agreed with me! So, where am I going with this? What could I have learned from such a beautiful, crazy, all-over-the-place day? Well, I thought about how my day started. We listened to our KMC church service. And then we listened to the pastor in a church in Florida where our daughter goes. One sermon was about how our precious God knows us intimately, intricately, immediately, and intentionally. He knows everything about us. And the other sermon was about how we are to bear fruit and that sometimes God must prune the "branches" to make them more productive. And while that can be painful, through it all, God is our only source of true joy. So, combining the two sermons... No matter the circumstance you find yourself in, God knows us better than anyone, and even if it is a tough time, God really is the source of our inner joy no matter what!

So, after "church," I went to be outside in God's amazing nature. Enjoying every bit of it.

The sun, the warmth, just the beauty in our walk. The beauty from our porch. The beauty of a mesmerizing fire. And the beautiful taste of roasted hot dogs! The beauty of getting to spend time with my husband! And especially, the beauty of God's amazing sky! But suddenly, there was darkness in the sky and the fearful push of the strong wind, which just threw us about physically and even emotionally. It made me think about how beautiful my life can be and how quickly things can happen that throw me for a loop! How do I manage tough, crazy, "catch me off guard" situations? Am I calm like my husband, trying to look at the whole picture to determine what is happening, or do I run around trying to catch all my "rugs" in fear of losing something I felt was so important to me? Sometimes after a situation is over, I realize how unimportant it was chasing after that "rug' with my life...compared to my actual life. It may be a silly example, but one that hit me. God longs for us to be with Him and show His love to others.

When we do not take time to do that, our lives can sometimes get tossed around to get our attention. It is a sort of pruning process. Something we cherish or spend a lot of time on may be taken away or ruined, and we cannot figure out why. But usually, when we can look back, we can see how God carried us through that time. And how we need to give God the glory for being there and guiding us through. So, my day went from meaningful to beautiful to more beautiful to scary, dark, and pushy, to gratifying, and back to meaningful again. Much like our lives can be many times. I need to learn to handle these ups and downs all in one day, or over a period, with grace, patience, and understanding. Remembering through any circumstance, God needs to always be my number one priority. I cannot go running after things that really don't matter. And if I can keep my focus on God and keep Him first, no matter what, He will bless me with true internal joy. Something no twister in life can take away. I am praying this can make sense to anyone who needs it and help them find that internal joy God so dearly wants us to have. To God be the Glory!

Joy that cannot be stolen!

Good Day

Sometimes I get so overwhelmed by thinking of all the things I need and want to do. I can ruin my whole day thinking about what I have to do tomorrow! It is crazy. As I thought about this, I realized that God has addressed that so long ago. Even in Bible times, people got overwhelmed. They had it so much harder just to do the basics of life. We have it harder because of all the extra stuff we put on ourselves. I had a crazy busy last couple of weeks. And it went so amazingly well I was surprised. I didn't feel extremely overwhelmed. Extremely tired...yes...but not overwhelmed. I realized I tried to take one day at a time like God said we should. It is really an amazing concept. Will I fall again and get all crazy when I am too busy? There's always that chance because I am human. But I am going to try to be more aware of God's advice. He only intended for us to deal with life one day at a time. So that is what I'm trying to do. Make one good day at a time. Choose joy one day at a time. Which hopefully can turn into a whole bunch of good, joyful days in a row! I must remember every time I choose to follow God's words, it always goes better. Those are my thoughts for today. I will think about tomorrow's thoughts tomorrow. But for now, I will go sit on my porch chair for a bit and remember my blessings and give my worries to God. And let tomorrow take care of itself... tomorrow! To God be the glory.

~Image by Lorie

Who Writes My Story?

Some days I find myself wondering what I am doing with my life. Other days I feel like God is completely in control. And yet others, I wonder why I'm being attacked, and nothing goes right. I heard someone say once that when we feel like we are being overwhelmed with tragedies of one kind or another, we need to remember who writes our story. When we allow God to be our author, we will not end in that defeated place. God will never leave us, and if we overcome our difficult situations allowing God to lead us through them, we will see the victory God intended for our story. So, on days that seem full of defeat, I will remember God writes my story. From beginning to end. And beyond.

I am forever grateful that I can give it all to Him and have peace through the trials. He knows me. He knows where He is going with my story. And my faith in Him helps me get through those challenging times with peace. It is such a blessing to be able to know that because God is writing my story, I have nothing to fear because He will write it just as it should be. (He authored the bestselling book ever…I'm OK with Him writing my story!) And that increases my faith so much. Even when I cannot see tomorrow, He can. And that is all I need to know to be able to live my life with joy. To God be the Glory!

Dear Lord,

Thank you for writing my story. For knowing every detail of my life. And for walking with me through it all. I am grateful to have you as my autobiographer. That gives me peace.

In Your Holy Name,

Amen

~Image by Lorie

Life Is Precious

This is something I think all of us know deep down. But life can also be frustrating. Stressful. Too busy. And downright exhausting. I remember thinking when our kids were still at home, I could not wait for a break. I was working full time, and the kids had needs and things they participated in that I wanted to be a part of. And for me, a lot of that time, I was extremely sick with horrible sinus issues and infections which eventually led to having a kidney transplant. I remember getting 2-3 hours of sleep a night, just trying to keep up with everything.

How I wish I could go back and relive that period of my life knowing what I know now. (I am sure I'm not alone there!) So how do we get past all the frustrations of life and remember how incredible this life is? If I could go back to the same circumstances, I would give it all to God and enjoy living more. I would not have just tried to get through the day. I would have enjoyed all the little moments. I am not saying I didn't enjoy anything, but I would have enjoyed everything about the kids and Marv. I would not have complained so much. And I certainly would not have worried about the little stuff...like how my house looked etc. The older I get, the more I realize what a wonderful life I have been given. Wonderful kids, an amazing husband, and now uniquely beautiful grandkids. And even with all the rough times, I am truly blessed. I have asked God for forgiveness. I did not realize at the time how great life was, and I thanked Him for all He had done in my life. I think when I was younger, I thought my life had to be perfect to be good.

As I get older, I realize it is not about how tired I am, or how frustrated I might be, or how many demanding times I go through. It is about how I manage all that. Do I include God to help me through? Do I remember that kindness always matters? Do I remember that how I act is a direct reflection of God? Sometimes when I am feeling sentimental and wishing that I could go back and do things differently, God reminds me I can still live like that now. It is never too late to change. So that is what I am trying to do. But for those young moms out there, I would say, do not let the frustrations be greater than the joys of your kids and the many blessings God has given you. Give all of that to God. You will be amazed at what He can do with it. I know you may think that is easy for me to say now, but I do know, in my heart, it truly is worth it. To God be the glory.

Dear Lord,

Thank you for all my life. Thank you for my wonderful husband. Amazing kids, incredible grandkids, and beautiful family and friends. Help me to now live my life enjoying the people you have put in my path, rather than getting frustrated or being too busy to enjoy them. I also pray for all the young mothers out there, that they will turn to you with their concerns and frustrations. That they learn earlier than I did that You are there for them. And that You care and love them so much that You are willing to take all those burdens on Your shoulders and turn them into good.

In Your Miraculous Name,

Amen

~Image by Lorie

Sit Still Lorie

I was once again enjoying this beautiful day God had blessed us with outside on our porch. And I almost had to start laughing!! Do you have any idea how much I used to dislike sitting and doing nothing? Seemed like such a waste of time! Marv loves to sit and think on the porch, on the deck, by the fire pit, or at the ocean! Anywhere he could find. He genuinely appreciates nature. And I always said I did too.

But the ocean was the only place I ever really enjoyed sitting because at least I felt like I was doing something. I was vacationing! I love nature, but never sat long enough to appreciate it like Marv does. Now, I am sure that is normal, to not just sit when you are a mom of three kids involved in things, working full time, and have a crazy busy life to deal with. It never seemed worthy of just sitting and enjoying what God has put before me. At least it was not an option for me. I mean, I had things to do. Important things. And at the time, they were important to me and to our family. But now...now I am sitting here, noticing that there are ten birds sitting right in front of me. Two robins, three red-wing blackbirds, a few sparrows, and some I can't identify. Wow. That is something. Ten years ago, I would have never noticed that. So, is that a good thing? Or is my life so boring that I am just the next old person to sit on the porch for something to do? (That one was extremely hard to put in writing!) But then I realized. Just as God says in His mighty word, there is a time for every season, I suppose He saves this incredibly special season for last. A period when we can have the time to deeply appreciate all He has given us. A time to give us a taste of Heavens beauty. I pray it will be a long season, so I can keep growing closer to Him in this beautiful nature He has provided. (I just got an Amen from a bullfrog!!) I also pray that I will be able to enjoy every song from a bird, and croak from a bullfrog. Notice every beautiful, colorful flower in front of me. Every nest of baby birds that gets built on our porch! And be able to praise God for this amazing world I am currently in, and for the incredible eternity He has provided for us to look forward to. To God be the glory!

~Image by Marv

Strength in God

Chapter 9

What a mighty God we have.

His love is amazing.

He gives me strength.

Through Him, I can do

anything.

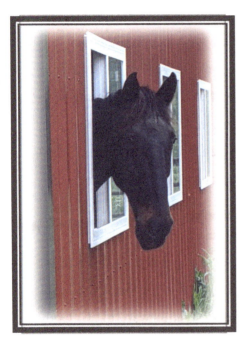

~Image by Marv

A Full Life

I remember thinking I just had to be a good person when I was younger. If I could just do that, God and others would love me, and my life would be great. And for quite some time, I lived like that ... struggling every day to be "perfect." Don't get me wrong, that is not a horrible goal. But it is an extremely frustrating and unattainable one. At least, that is what I found it to be. I would do my best to do everything right, and then I would spend my days worrying about how I did things wrong. It is an exhausting life. It was not until I was in my late 30s that I honestly started understanding I didn't have to live like that. God was working on my heart, showing me that perfection was not only not necessary, but it was not attainable. God showed me, little by little, that believing and trusting in Him was the goal I needed to work towards. And in doing that, I have found fullness in life. Do I get discouraged? Yes, I am human, so, of course, sometimes I do. But it takes me less time to realize God has this every time. He has got this life of mine. And I know where I am going when I die, and that leads to such a sense of peace in life. My desire now is to share that peace with as many people as I can so they may experience the fullness of life that God desires for all of us.

To know the beauty of God. The wonder of God. The peace of knowing God. He is trustworthy. He is faithful. He is kind. He is just. He is loving. And He is my Savior. And knowing that makes my life full. And that is my prayer for everyone. To God be the glory.

Dear Lord,

Today I am so thankful for the lessons You have taught me. Even the painful ones... especially those that have helped me have a full life. A life that has peace because I know where I am going when I am no longer here. Today I am praying for You to please touch the hearts of many people and give them peace. Peace in knowing You so they can have the fullness in life You desire for them to have. I pray this peace will let them sleep like a baby, knowing they are in your hands...always. That is true peace.

Amen

Decision Making

There are so many ways to make decisions. There is the "Wing it" decision maker. Then comes the "Creative Wing It" decision maker (which I used to be and can tend to lean that way). There is the "Thoughtful" decision maker (my husband). And there is the "OVER Thoughtful" decision maker (sometimes my husband). But last, of all, there is the "Spirit Led" decision maker. (I fluctuate between this and the creative wing it).

So, what is the difference? Well, the "wing it" will see something and think, why not? Let's give it a whirl. Sometimes it works. Sometimes it does not. The worst we can do is fail.

The "creative wing it" sees an opportunity and thinks, I could make that work if I did this and that, and then says, let's go for it. If we fail, we will try again. They have better chances than a regular "wing it" because there is some thought about how they, as a human, could make it work. But certainly not a sure thing. The "thoughtful" will put much thought into it. They will look at it, crunch some numbers, and make an informed human decision. And then decide yes or no. (It feels like the safest HUMAN route to go) The "OVER thoughtful" will crunch numbers until there is no way it could work, playing devil's advocate in every scenario and talking themselves out of trying anything new... maybe ever. (No way to live). But... the "Spirit led" will see an opportunity that they feel in their gut will work, then pray about it and truly put it in God's hands to open the doors that are needed. And to close those doors that need to stay closed (What an amazing way to live). One catch... you need to have patience and faith.

God's timing is not always our own, but always perfect. The good news? Pray and let it go. Live your life in between and wait for God to work His miracles. A warning about this method... it often seems unsafe and may make no sense at all, but in God's upside-down kingdom, it makes perfect sense. Waiting is not always easy, but it is worth it. So, take it for what it's worth. I have found that God gets it right every time. Being a "Spirit led" decision-maker has changed my life and could change yours as well if you can overcome the fear and the advice of well-meaning humans who do not understand God's plan for your life. There is so much truth to the saying..." Let go and let God. ". He will never let you down. To God be the glory.

Dear Lord,

Thank you for always knowing what is best for my life and never letting me down. I am so grateful that even when things don't go as I would plan, I can look back on my life and see how You have ALWAYS worked things out for my good and Your glory.

In Your Holy Name,

Amen

~ Image by Marv

Freedom for Your Soul

I do not know about you, but I used to wonder how your soul could have freedom. It is a weird thought. But as I have lived my life, I have come to realize it revolves around God. Like anything else in life! There have been times in my life when I have been in torment over something that happened. I could work my soul into a frenzy because I did something wrong. Or someone I loved was hurt. Or I did something just plain weird, and people saw me do it! I was embarrassed or afraid someone thought I did something stupid. I might have thought people were going to talk about me behind my back. (My daughter pointed out to me that it was very conceited to think they took time to talk about me!) So, of course, then I did not want people to think I was conceited. It could go on and on. But when I realized putting my trust and faith in God gave me such peace, it was like my soul had this freedom. I realized that was the key. The key to releasing the torment that life in this world can bring.

If things happen that I do not understand. Trust God. I make mistakes... even big ones. Trust God. Someone I love passes away. Trust God. Politics!! That is a tough one these days. Trust God. Loved ones go through huge tragedies in their life, and I stand by watching it while feeling helpless. Trust God. The pattern here is that once I put my trust in God, all that torment just magically goes away. It leaves because I do not doubt God controls all this crazy life. All He asks of me is to trust Him completely. God is such an amazing God. There is such peace and freedom in that. Right down to the depths of my soul. To God be the glory!

~Image by Marv

Life Blood

I am not becoming a mystery writer, and I realize this could sound like a very gruesome topic! But it is quite the opposite. When I think of the blood Jesus sacrificed for me, I can hardly believe it. I know what Jesus went through could be called gruesome because it was. But the beauty of the blood is just too amazing of a story to overlook. And sometimes, I think we, as intelligent humans, are hesitant to believe something so incredible. We can always logically talk ourselves out of it being true. And I think many people who are very intellectual find themselves doing just that. How can we begin to wrap our minds around this beautiful gift from God? I grew up in a Christian home and never really questioned what had been done for me until I got older.

I remember going through some times when I tried to understand how God could have done such an amazing thing, only to confuse myself with logic. I realized the enormity of God's gift when I went through the first huge valley in my life. I was amazed at how He so masterfully carried me through and increased my faith. There were no other explanations for the things that came about in my life exactly when I needed them, except it was God. That was such an unbelievably valuable lesson and one I will never regret having to go through to learn. God knew exactly what he was doing! So, for the record, I hate the sight of blood. My kids will attest to that. Marv always had to help them when there was blood involved! But even so, the blood of Jesus is one I can absolutely love. He went through so much for each of us that I cannot imagine how he must have felt. I want to always remember the blood that Jesus shed for me when He made the journey to the cross. And I never want to take the beauty and meaning of it all for granted! What an amazing God we have! To God be the glory!

~Image by Lorie

Our Massive God

I heard someone say the word massive today. For some reason, it really jumped out at me. It got me thinking about how massive God is. How massive His love is for us. How massive His arms must be to reach around any of us who seek Him... all at the same time. How massive His creativity must be to create this amazing world...the animals, the flowers, the mountains, the ocean.

One day, while at the ocean, Marv and I saw pelicans up close, and I was amazed at their wingspan. They are magnificent birds and fun to watch. We stood there as one was coming straight at us then flew back away. He spread out his massive wings, and I thought about the number of times God has come to swoop me up and put out His massive, loving arms to carry me or just let me know He loves me. So, I have decided massive is a huge word, no pun intended. It is a word that, when looked at closely, we need to pay attention to because it describes so much of God. I am so thankful for a massive God. One who loves me so much He sent His only son to hold my massive sin. So much, there is no other word that can fully describe the amount of love God has for us...except massive. To God be the glory.

Dear Lord,

Please never let me forget that You are massive enough to be everywhere at the same time. Or that Your love and forgiveness for me is so massive that nothing could ever take me from You... except my own bad decisions. Thank you, Lord, for being so massively amazing. My love only grows more massive for You every day.

In Your Name,

Amen

~Images by Marv

Power in Your Name

As I was driving today, I heard the Christian song "Power in Your Name," which got me thinking about power. There are so many people fighting for power these days, and I cannot quite wrap my head around it all. Politics are ridiculous. People doing things they would not normally do just to get ahead in Washington. Big businesses do not really treat their employees with kindness anymore. Everyone wants to make it up the ladder. And when they get to the top, they feel the power instead of remembering who really makes a business successful. I suppose it is a human desire embedded in some of us to want to have power. Be in control. I am sure there were times I have been guilty of wanting power over something. But I can honestly say I have no desire for that anymore. I realize how blessed I am that God is in control of my life. He has power over me. And there is power in His name alone.

At least the kind of power that matters. I am so thankful for that. And I wish that for so many people. To have peace knowing that God is here for you. And to know His power is endless on your behalf is an amazing feeling.

One feeling I truly wish for everyone. Especially my family. But anyone out there that is searching, I am praying today that you will find God's incredible peace. To God be the Glory!

~Image by Marv

Shades of Slavery

I was listening to Zach Williams's song, "No Longer Slaves," and the thought of being a slave came to my mind. What am I a slave to? He talks about being a slave to fear in his song. And that used to be something I had to fight against. What if this happens to me? What if something bad happens to Marv or my kids? Or my grandkids? I can remember being fearful of all that and much more. But when I faced kidney failure, God showed me so clearly how He would walk with me through anything. I am sure some of you have also experienced a similar time in your life when you would say, "All I could do" was trust God. And I said that as though it was not enough! Trust me, it is absolutely enough!

However, as I walked through my kidney journey with God by my side, I soon realized it was not "all I could do," but rather, it was "all I ever needed to do." Trusting God in all circumstances brings such freedom to life.

I realized that sometimes I enslave myself to fear because of my own bad choices. But what I have learned, without a doubt, is that I am a child of God. And God is the best father I will ever have. He will never forsake me or leave me. There will be times in life I may want to ask God, "Why me?" But then, God shows me once again; He is all I ever need to get me through life and death and bring me to eternal life.

What an incredible way to break out of any circumstance that holds us as slaves. Mountain or valley, God is always by my side. And He can be by your side too if you choose to let Him. Right now, I am on a mountaintop on vacation where struggling to be a slave to chocolate milkshakes is my biggest concern. I know there will be times again when there will be far more critical issues than this. But God is walking with me now. And I know He will walk with me when it is a different time in my life and I'm walking through a valley. God is good. He is loving. He is kind. And he is always faithful. To God be the glory!

Dear Lord,

Thank you for this mountaintop time in my life. Help me to remember that while You are walking with me now, You will also be there with me no matter what valley I may have to walk through. Please do not allow me to become a slave to fear. Help me to enjoy the mountaintops and be grateful for Your presence in the valleys. Thank you, Lord, for being faithful.

In Your Faithful Name,

Amen

~Image by Marv

Swimming Through the Fog

This morning the fog was thick out over Lake Placid, Florida. Watching the ducks, I am amazed at how confidently they move through the thick fog. They do not look confused or worried. They simply move forward with complete faith that the water will be there even if they cannot see it. I am guessing a lot of you are like me and have a few days here and there feeling like you are "in a fog." I think the next time I am feeling a little "foggy," I will try to remember those ducks and how calm they were swimming through it.

There was a day I would have been panicky and afraid when going through rough times, but just like the ducks, I have found I am able to have faith. For me, it is faith in my Lord and Savior. That He will lead me while I am in the fog and carry me through those hard times.

So much to be thankful for. Especially the times he has lifted me up and shown me the way through to the sun. So, taking a quote from Dory in Finding Nemo, "Just keep swimming." God will be there with you if you put your faith in Him. To God be the glory!

Dear Lord,

I pray for peace when going through the fog of my life. Help me to remember the ducks and how calm they remained even when they could not see where they were going. You are such an amazing God and so greatly to be praised. Your mighty hand covers me when needed and welcomes me into the sun when I get there. Thank you, Lord, for Your infinite love and concern for me.

In Your Holy Name,

Amen

~Image by Marv

Who's Your Landlord?

I heard someone talk this morning about allowing God to be the Lord over our "land." And if we do, when things go wrong, He will fix it. It is very frustrating if we insist on having control over our own life because we think we must fix things ourselves. I thought, wow. That applies to so many areas of my life. Everything I have belongs to God. My finances. My thoughts. My material things. I only have these because God has blessed me with them. It is so important for me to remember this. As soon as I put so much pride into the things I "own," life can start to fall apart. I am not saying we shouldn't work hard or enjoy what we have. But for me, God has ways of reminding me that we are just passing through this world. And God is not going to ask me how many things I have accumulated on this earth. Or if they were the best brand names.

But He will want to know how I treated others. And if I was ever willing to share His love with those who needed it. So, I was thinking about landlords. And I am so thankful I have the best "Landlord" of all in Jesus. He already knows when things happen in my life that need fixing. Since all I have is from Him, He already has a plan on how to fix it. And since He lives in my heart, He is even landlord of ME! What an incredible burden that takes off my shoulders. What more could you ask for? To God be the glory.

Life is grand when we give it all to God…

You are Chosen

When I think of being chosen, I think of someone who is above others. They have a reason to stand out because of their talents. Maybe they are chosen for sports. They are athletically above other people's abilities and are chosen in the sports arena. Or musically inclined and they excel in this. Maybe they have a high IQ and therefore are admired in the intellectual world. Perhaps someone has an outstanding mind for business and is "chosen" among the business elites. Or perhaps they are very wealthy because of good financial choices, and they are admired in the world of finance.

Whatever the case, people are usually chosen because of a talent they were born with or acquired through much hard work. But this is not the case in God's world. We are all "chosen." All we are required to do is choose God in return. No special talents needed. No reason to keep an account of all our accomplishments. No resume needed. God does not look at the list of what we have done while we were in this world. He simply looks at our hearts. He may look at how we treat others. Or if we helped those in need around us. But most of all, He will look at our hearts to see how much we honored Him. How much we feared Him. How much faith we had in Him. How much we truly loved Him and others. It is amazing if you think about it. It is the only place in this crazy world we can be chosen without being the best at a specific talent. All that is asked of us is to love God. To believe in Him with all our hearts. To recognize Him as our Savior. No huge skills are required. It is just there for the taking. All we need to do is accept this precious gift. I cannot think of anywhere else in this world that we can be accepted with such little to offer and, in return, have such blessed assurance. What an amazing God we worship. And to Him be the Glory!

Dearest Lord,

Thank you, Lord, for allowing me to choose You, and for choosing me. Thank you for all the blessings you have given me. I pray today that anyone who has not chosen You as their Savior will understand that You have already chosen them. All they need to do is respond. You have this beautiful life of peace and security to offer them. I pray their hearts will open. And Lord, on days I find it difficult to remember all Your many blessings or feel Your peace, please remind me of all of it. You are an amazing God and I have no reason to fear because You are not only in control of my life, but my entire world. Thank you for that! Today and every day, Lord, I choose You!

In Your Everlasting name,

Amen

~Image by Marv

Character Thoughts

I read that our character is totally determined by what we do when no one is looking. We (including me!) fail to remember that God is always watching. Whether I like it or not. I am being convicted to remember that today. And when I remember that one big fact, it changes my way of doing things. Not just when I am in public, and I want to make sure I look like a good person. Not just when I am around my church family, and I want to be sure they all know I'm saved and going to Heaven. But I want to be the same person at home and everywhere.

I am not saying that's how I've always been. Not by a long shot. I have failed miserably at times. And if we were all honest, I think we would all have to admit to that. But I am saying I want to strive to live for an audience of one. By doing that, I think the rest will come naturally. And then, only then can we bring the glory to God that He so rightfully deserves. We have an impressive leader in God. We do not ever have to wonder if he is corrupt or will attack us somehow. He gives us true freedom. And that is an unmeasurable gift these days. Let's live our lives for Him. And lean on Him to take care of the issues in a way only He can do. And always remember… He is watching us because He loves us! Not to judge us. To God be the glory!

~Image by Marv

Walking In the Spirit

I have heard it said before: "The true test of walking in the Spirit will not be in the way we act, but in the way we react to the daily frustrations of life."

This really hit home for me. I am sure many of you would have to admit, along with me, how easy it is to get frustrated. A car in front of me is going too slow. Or a car cut me off. Or they take the parking spot I was waiting for. A person in front of me in the checkout line picked up something with no price on it. The kids are whining all day. Someone at work just gets under my skin. Our spouses are not acting like we think they should. The list could go on and on.

All those small, but irritating things can make us react like rabid dogs. And for what reason? As if those are not bad enough, now we move on to the big things! Our world. Our government. Our churches. Our skin colors. Our rights. Our freedoms. Our lack of justice today. Our opinion is not being heard. These important things matter to us while we are in this world. But do any of them truly matter eventually? Especially so much that we react in a way that hurts others. As the quote I wrote earlier says, it is not always about how we act but how we react. I think it is easy for most of us to do something kind for someone who needs it. Christian or not, that is something we, as humans, have the empathy to do for someone. But when something is done to us that we perceive as a grievance, that is when it matters how we react. I have failed miserably at this many times and am terribly sorry for acting the way I did in certain instances. But I do believe that how we respond when something happens that we feel is wrongful to us; that is when we can see someone truly filled (or not) with the Holy Spirit. I am striving to become better at this. And the best way to do that is to fill my heart and my head with God's word. Easier said than done sometimes. But at the very least, after what God has done for me, He deserves my honest effort to keep in touch with Him and to grow more like Him every day. To God be the glory!

Dear Lord,

Please fill me with Your Holy Spirit. Give me the resolve to visit with You every day and hear what You would have me do that day. Please help me continually desire to fill my head and heart with Your words and Your characteristics so I can become more like You. I want to be able to react to hard circumstances with faith and grace rather than hate and hurt.

In Your Precious Name,

Amen

~Image by Marv

The Journey Home

Chapter 10

For me, the ultimate home

I can have will be in Heaven.

These are thoughts

about loved ones who now

permanently live in Heaven!

Our Very Own Ronald McDonald

My sister, Diane, married someone named Ron. It turned out he became this incredibly important part of our family. When our kids were little, they called him Uncle Ronald McDonald. And to this day, they sometimes catch themselves saying it. He was fun, full of life, and always there to help. And he, in turn, made up names for some of our kids. The most famous one was what he called our son, Alex… "The Alex Meister." We even had it put on one of Alex's birthday cakes. I can still see Ron's face when he saw it. Priceless. He just wanted to make the kids feel special.

He also worked with Marv in Marv's sports store for a few years. And he became the brother to Marv that he never had. Sometimes God just puts people in our paths that we will never forget. Ron was one of those people, not just because he was our brother-in-law, but because he cared so much about us. Our families went on trips together when the kids were younger. The four of us often went out and saw what we could get into. It could be from getting ice cream to going to Florida together. We loved going out to eat together. Ron would always sit down, inspect the napkin, and then look at the menu to see what kind of shrimp he wanted to get. He examined the napkin because that was how he rated restaurants. He needed large napkins, trust me. So, if they had soft, skimpy napkins that was a problem. Even now, when we see a big napkin at a restaurant, we say, "Ron would have loved this place." We have so many great memories of our times together. He was also very giving, helpful, and always there for others. There was a period when I was waiting for my transplant, Marv built furniture out of pallets in his workshop to bring in some extra money.

Ron finally retired and would show up almost daily to help Marv. Sometimes that was just being there to talk and keep Marv on track; other times, he would get in there and work. But I can still see him walking in our door with his little lunchbox like he was going to work. He always knew how to make us laugh. Marv and he would have "bro" dates. It was a joke with our kids. Why does Dad go on more dates with Ron than you? But I am so glad they were able to do that. He was indeed a blessing for Marv. They went to many sporting events and whatever Ron could come up with. He loved planning things to do.

Unfortunately, soon after their 45th anniversary, Ron became extremely sick. He was diagnosed with a rare blood cancer. He went downhill quickly for the next 5 months, from October 2017 until February 2018. We were scheduled to go to Florida in February for our winter getaway. We were very hesitant to go, but Ron insisted, "Go! Do not stay here because of me." We went. But he and Diane were always on our minds. We had not been there very long when we got a call from our niece, Rachel that Ron was not doing well. She had flown home from Seattle, and he was in the hospital.

We immediately got in the car and drove home to be there, not just for Ron, but for Diane and their family. It was soon evident that he would not be here with us much longer. He finally went home from the hospital with Hospice coming in to help. He was not eating very much anymore. But we asked him, "What can we get you to eat, Ron? Anything sound good?" and of course, he said, "I could eat some shrimp." We got in the car and got him some shrimp with large napkins. He sat up in the chair as best he could and ate some shrimp. Not a lot, but just enough to help him remember how good it was. A day or so after that, we got a call from Rachel saying, please come over, Dad's not ok. We went right over, and they were all in the bedroom with Ron. The hospice nurse was there and just trying to keep him comfortable. As I watched every breath, he tried so hard to take, it was as if he couldn't give up. Something was on his mind. But the pain and hurt of seeing him like that brought tears to everyone's eyes.

We were all at that place, we did not want to let him go, but we didn't want him to continue hurting. Diane backed away from him for a minute, and I stepped close to him and whispered in his ear, "Diane will be fine. We will all be here for her." When I backed away, he settled down and became very peaceful. We all looked at each other, like, is that it? There is the initial response of, NO, please don't go... to thank you God, we're so glad he isn't hurting anymore. He simply cared to the end about my sister. He wanted to be sure she would be OK. And once he heard someone say she would be ok, he was able to let go. That is often the case when someone is on their deathbed. They need to know its ok for them to meet their maker. We were so blessed to be there at that moment. Marv was incredibly close to Ron. We all got a chance to say our goodbyes in our own ways. And that was important for Marv and me. But, more importantly, his whole family, Diane, Rachel, and his son Aaron were able to be there and say their goodbyes also. To this day, we miss him terribly.

Sometimes something will remind me of him, and I will burst out laughing. What a blessing to have known him. And we cannot wait to meet him again in Heaven!

~Images by Lorie

Never Ending Smile and Love

That was my sister-in-law-Janice. She had one of the kindest hearts of anyone I ever knew. As I was completing my book, she very unexpectedly passed away. She created a huge hole here on earth, but God got an amazing angel that day. She had a quiet sense of humor that seemed as though she did not even know how funny she was. I think the best way to describe Janice was she was a sweet, sweet, soul. And her heart very much broke for others who were hurting. Family was important to her. She and my brother Stan made a concerted effort to stop and see our daughter and son-in-law when they were in Florida. She was always interested in how they were doing. She would often text and I enjoyed texting with her. She would ask about our kids and always show concern for what they were going through.

I was the flower girl in their wedding 55 years ago. She made me feel so special because that is just what Janice did…she loved people and always thought of them before herself. And the way she and Stan stood by each other was a remarkable sight. They were truly in love, even after 55 years of marriage. It was like it was still their honeymoon.

She passed away very quickly. Which made me happy for her that she did not have to suffer. But for the rest of us, especially Stan and their family, it made it extremely hard. There is that feeling of complete shock that accompanies a death like this. When one minute you are playing games with family and the next you are gone. How is one supposed to deal with that kind of loss? The only way I know is with God. He has a way of carrying us through something like this. He can give us good memories when we do not think we can even smile. He can bring hints of joy when we least expect it. I pray that will be the case for my brother and his family. And because we know Janice will be in heaven, this truly isn't goodbye…it's just we will see you later! What a reunion that will be!

I remember Janice saying to me more than once, I wish we (all us siblings and families) could just build houses together and have our own little community! Well Janice, we will join you someday and then maybe we can have that!

Until then, say hello to Mom, Dad, Larry, and Ron for us. We know you are in God's hands! To God be the glory!

Their 50th Anniversary…loving like they just got married.

Life, Death, And Beyond

My sister-in-law, Mary called this morning with sad news. My brother Larry passed away. He was at peace and is at peace now. I thought about how we all talk about someone being in Heaven when they pass away. It is a most comforting thought and is said almost always when someone dies. But, with Larry, I know that I know that is where he is, and that brings such peace for me. Life, death, and beyond. I know not everyone believes the same things I do. I am simply saying what my heart feels right now. I think that life on this earth is short and worth living each day.

1) Larry's life... he was always full of life. He knew how to make us laugh. He knew how to make me feel loved. Did he fail at times? Yep. He sure did. So have I. But Larry came to know Jesus as his savior, and he cherished his Savior for his last number of years.

2) Death...No one really likes that word, and understandably so, because we think of what we will be missing in this life. Our spouses, children, grandchildren, and just family and friends in general. But with God, what a future we have. I am so glad Larry was at peace and resting comfortably when he died. I have created this image

in my mind of our mom standing in Heaven with her arms open wide and a big smile to greet the son she prayed so dearly for and always believed in. What a moving image that is.

3) Then the beyond. That is where we can all differ in what we believe. I talked a few times with Larry about God. And I know that is where he knew he was going…to Heaven. And I am positive that is where he is now.

Larry was the brother that never looked at me as the annoying little sister. I was the youngest of 6 children with a span of 16 years between me and my oldest sibling. When everyone else ran for the hills if I came around, Larry would pay attention to me.

I love you, Larry, and as I was sitting here on Coquina Beach, videoing the ocean, this lone person walked through. I imagined that it was you, Larry. Calm, being in nature, peaceful, and going for a walk. Thanks for being a good brother. All my love.

Dear Precious Lord,

I pray today that many people can learn from my brother's life and mine. Perfection is not required or even expected by You, Lord. I thank you from the bottom of my heart for that. But with You, we have a chance to be perfectly imperfect through your son. Thank you for loving us. Thank you for touching my heart. And thank you for touching Larry's heart. He is in Your hands now.

In Your Holy Name,

Amen

~Image by Lorie

I am so glad you are at peace Larry!

Larry was an amazing umpire.

My Quiet Father

As I wrote before about my dad, he was a quiet man. Deep thinking. Kind. And very quiet. But his eyes! They smiled all by themselves! I loved my dad a lot. I remember when he passed away. He had been in the nursing home for a few years. He had Parkinson's disease and could not remember a lot at that point. When my daughter Abby and I visited him, he would think she was me. He would call her Loretta…he was the only person who ever called me that. My daughter and I do look very much alike. But then, he had no clue who I was. It was extremely hard to visit him. I knew it was not him. But it was hard when he did not even know me.

Around Thanksgiving in 1999, my family was gathered for a thanksgiving meal at our house. My mom was there, and the phone rang. It was the nursing home calling to say Dad was not doing very well. He ended up in the hospital. The nurses were truly kind and put 2 beds together so Mom and he could sleep side by side. They knew he would not last a long time.

Several years earlier, I wrote a poem for my dad for Father's Day. I had someone I knew who did calligraphy write it on parchment paper and then frame it for him. I remember being so excited to give it to him. He really appreciated it. After all, at least it was not another Father's Day tie! The poem went like this:

Remember when storms would come,

and I was afraid, how you made me laugh.

Or you wanted me to wear pigtails and braids...

but I was too old for that.

Or when I wanted something really bad,

mom would say to ask you,

and you would say...ask your mom.

Or you would tease me,

the way only you could do, and I would fight it

and scream about it...then tease you back.

But of everything to remember,

something that will always hold true,

is of all the dads in all the world,

the best has got to be you!

Now as I sat with him in the hospital knowing he would soon be gone, I wanted to write another poem. This is what was in my heart that day...

Dad, we're both older now.

 I sit and watch you grasp for every breath.

The doctor says you could leave us anytime. I wait.

     I wonder. When?

I watch mom as she sits by your bed and talks to you...

     hoping you can hear...

     believing you can hear.

I watch as all our family comes to visit you...

     the love is so great, and I understand why my children,

     on their own, decide to come see you and give

     Grandma Lehman hugs. I see them help me at home,

     so I don't have to worry...the generations carry on.

This is what you and mom have started...

     a family who cares and remembers.

I still remember the pigtails, the storms, the love

     you gave me. I remember your gentleness,

     the twinkle in your eye, and especially your smile.

Now as I stroke your hair, I hope you can feel,

through my hands, a little of the love you gave me.

And I still know, of everything to remember,

something that will always hold true,

is of all the dads in all the world,

the best has got to be you.

I love you Dad…always.

~Image by J Augspurger

Sweet Grandma Lehman

As I sit here and think about why we celebrate Mother's Day, I of course, first think of my mom. She was an amazing lady. She raised six kids, four incredibly ornery boys, and two precious girls. There is sixteen years difference between my oldest brother and me. I am sure I didn't see my mom do all the same things my siblings did that grew up closer in age. I potentially was a little more spoiled. Mom was forty-two when I was born, so by the time I was a teenager, she was kind of tired. I am sure saying yes to things came a bit easier. Do not get me wrong. She still let me know right from wrong. But some of it I figured out the hard way. I am pretty sure I just plain got away with a little more than my siblings. But I have so much love for my mom. She might not have been the most educated or bold woman in the world. But she sure knew how to love someone unconditionally. Her heart was about as big as they come. She never stopped caring or praying for her family and friends. I will be forever grateful for the way she showed us how to love. I always knew my mom was there. Even when she lived into her nineties, she still had her prayer lists in her Bible. And every day, she would lift everyone on that list up in prayer. I have these lists to this day to remind me of the importance of prayer. I was thinking, I really cannot ask for more than that. She knew how to laugh. She loved chocolate and sweet things! The only time I ever saw her get "mean" was when we played games. She was a little competitive! But if I had the choice of an educated, rich, feminist woman or my mom, mom would win every time because she taught me about what was necessary. Putting God first. She was affectionately called Grandma Lehman; we still talk about her to this day. My grandkids (even the ones that never met her) still talk about Grandma Lehman. But something that really affected me was when she passed away. And I want to share this with you because it was an absolute miracle. I could have never imagined this. We were at our daughter's wedding in Florida when she went into the hospital. We got through the wedding with tears of happiness and sorrow at the same time. We raced home as soon as we could after the reception and made it home on Sunday evening. She went into the hospital on Thursday. Friends we knew, who worked in the hospital where she was, had communicated to us that it was not good. She had not spoken since Friday, but I was glad to be there so I could talk to her. I stayed with her every night. Everyone grieves differently, and for me, it was just so important I be there.

Monday, I was talking to the doctor because I hated seeing her starving. I know this is how it works towards the end. I realize you just aren't hungry at this point, and it probably was harder for me than her. But the doctor said, what does she like?" I immediately said, "Chocolate." He laughed and said, "Well, give her some. It's fine!" My friend who was with me had a piece of chocolate, and I put it under her tongue. Now remember, she had not been responsive for days. But at that moment, she sat straight up in bed, looked right at me, and said, "I love you!" Then laid back down. That was unnerving. But I know for Mom if anything could do it, it was chocolate! My best friend was there with me then, and we just looked at each other like, did that just happen? What a gift I was given. Then by the time Wednesday rolled around, she was struggling so hard to breathe but just would not give up. As I looked at her, I thought, that does not look like Mom. She always cared about her hair. Looking nice was always important to her. So, I asked the nurse if I could wash and fix her hair. They graciously helped me dry wash it. I used a curling iron, teased it, and fixed it the best I could. Then I looked at her and said, "Now you're ready Mom." And it was not even five minutes, and she took her last breath. Knowing Mom, she just had to look her best to meet her Savior.

I cannot even explain the wonderful gifts God gave me during that time. I felt at peace. As though I could give her the little I could for the last time. I still miss her so much every day. I feel so blessed to have had her in my life. She may not have been educated, but she was wise about what mattered. I can only hope to be half as much of a woman of God as her. And now, I see our children starting to follow in her footsteps by putting God first in their lives, and I know what an influence she had on them. So do not ever say, "I'm just a stay-at-home mom." It truly is the most important job you will ever do. I wish I could have been home with my kids all the time. It has now been 11 years since she passed away. And on May 31st, 2023, she would have been 106 years old. But I am sure she looks better than ever in Heaven, spending time with those she loved who passed before her, by her side. And she is

waiting there to welcome all her family to Heaven. Today I am thankful for Moms, especially my mom, who I will love forever. To God be the Glory.

Grandpa Reuben

I had a wonderful Grandpa that used to stop by almost every day to see us. Mom would always make her rolled oats soup for breakfast, and we would usually be sitting there eating it when he would come in. I wanted to pay tribute to my grandpa Reuben. (My maternal grandpa). He was a kind soul and we all loved him very much.

I never knew my other real grandparents because they either died before I was born or when I was very young.

I took this picture below and wrote two poems to go with it. One is about Grandpa Reuben and one about my mom, Grandma Lehman. Then I framed them to give to my mom.

Grandpa Reuben

Grandpa, your clock chimes
To remind me of the times
you spent with me laughing,
sharing your values and caring.

The glasses remind me of the way
you saw things, with wisdom and love.

Your Bible is a reminder of your life
because everything you did was based
on God's word.

I miss you, Grandpa. The candy you used
to give me is a sweet reminder of a gentle
man who not only talked about God's love,
but spent his life sharing it. Thank you for
sharing it with me.

Grandma Lehman

The clock is now yours. My
children hear it at your house
when they visit. Someday it will
remind them of the laughter, love
and care you gave to them.

Your oil lamp reminds us of how
you let God's light shine.

The doile you made represents the
time you would take to do anything
for us. God first, then your family.
Grandpa's ways shine through you.

Time goes on. Each generation carries
the light in a different way. Thank you
for showing us the right way.

Great Grandma Troyer…

A "Great" Grandma

I always loved Jewell, my mother-in-law. She had a way about her that was not judgmental. She always made me feel welcome. When I had a chance to talk to her alone, I got to see her sense of humor. She was a hard worker and worked as a waitress almost up to when she unexpectedly passed away in May of 2007. She was from West Virginia and had her own language. The kids loved her very much, but they also enjoyed trying to speak (or harass her about) her "language." Kmart was Kmark. Oil was oral. Cereal was ceral. Davenport (couch) was a Damport! You get the picture. But she was a lot of fun and took it all in stride. We often said she and Grandpa could have made their own sitcom. It would have been a hit, I am sure. They would sit in their chairs in their living room and pick at each other. It was their way of showing love, I think. At least, that is what I always told myself. But the way they would banter back and forth was very comical. And always gave our kids a good laugh. She was very willing to help with the kids, which was such a blessing because my mom was older and could not do a lot of babysitting.

Grandma loved to buy lottery tickets. She won more than I would have ever imagined, but never won big! So, one Christmas, I found this "fake" lottery ticket I wrapped up for her. When she scratched it off and "won" $100,000, she started screaming, "Oh my goodness, oh my goodness. What am I going to do with all that money?" Then I felt terrible. I had to break the news to her that it was fake. As I am writing this down, it sounds kind of mean, but later she laughed as hard as we did. Especially when we looked at the video. She just needed time to forget everything she was going to use that money for. And it has now become a classic story! I had amazing parents-in-law. And for that, I am truly grateful. We still miss Jewell's laughter and her presence at family gatherings! And will always remember her with much love!

An Ode To

Great Grandpa Troyer

My father-in-law was another one of those people who could make you laugh when he wanted to. He was a favorite of our kids! Our three children were their only grandkids, so they got lots of attention. He was the kind of grandpa I would wait in suspense for the kids to return from his house, so I could see what ornery thing he taught them this time! He was always there for them. We lived just up the street from the elementary school. A short walk for the kids.

I walked to school when I was little and never felt it was bad for them to walk home, even in the rain. I did not think they would melt. But Grandpa Troyer would watch the weather, and I always knew when I was working, if it was even sprinkling, he would be there to pick them up. It was his way of showing them how much he loved them. We knew we could always count on him for anything he was able to do. If we were too busy, he would mow. When we had a yellow jacket nest in our house, he showed up with big gloves and multiple spray cans! It was comical to see him and Marv attack that nest. But they got it done! He helped Marv renovate our entire basement in our first house to make an office and family room that was well used. He also had an extremely ornery side which everyone loved. It was the kind of ornery you could see in his face. I don't know if I ever told him how much I really appreciated all he did for us. I would say thanks every time. But I hope he knew just how much we felt blessed to have him there! He lived quite a few years in remission from cancer, but then unfortunately, he died in October 2007, 4 months after Grandma Troyer died. He did have cancer, but I think he missed Grandma a lot and had a broken heart. We all miss his smile and that ornery look he had on his face. He was loved very much.

The Troyer Men

The End Game

I ask myself this often. What is the end game of life? Is it that I am wealthy with lots of money so I can impress people with my "worth"? Is it so people will remember how critical I was to society? Is it so they remember the great things I did? Is the end game to be so famous in this world that my name will always be remembered? Would that make me worth more? Indeed, my belongings and material things would be worth more money if I had been famous. But would it give me any more worth to God? Of course not. These may seem like very odd questions to even ask. But if I was to honestly answer those questions, I would have to say there was a time when those things were important to me. We all go through growing pains, and as God leads us through our lives, we realize the importance of the "end game." If you do not believe in God, I think the answer to all those questions could be a resounding yes. Because if this life is all there is and then it's over, I would want those things, too, while I am here. But what a peace there is when we know, as believers of God, that our "end game" truly includes no end. God gives us that beautiful choice to spend eternity with Him. He is saying we are ALL worthy. Worthy of this life and the next. Worthy of spending eternity in our Father's house. What if God could send out invitations to everyone to live with Him in eternity, and we just had to send back an RSVP? Would that make it a more realistic choice? But God does not even make us do that. We simply have to say yes and allow Him into our hearts. What an amazing game plan God came up with. If we choose Him, we really cannot lose. For that, I am so very thankful. To God be the glory! I wrote these personal stories about some of those close to us that have already made that journey home. It was healing for me to write about it. But I am hoping it might help someone out there that is grieving. I would encourage you to sit and think about all the wonderful, funny things you can remember about them. And have a little chuckle on their behalf. Laughter is a very healing medicine. And it is one medicine with only good side effects! Also, remember if they were believers, it is not goodbye…it is, I'll see you later!

Made in the USA
Monee, IL
08 February 2025

11892624R00134